THE CURIOUS TRAVELLER THROUGH LAKELAND

By the same author

THREE RIVERS

OFF TO THE LAKES

OFF TO THE DALES

LANCASHIRE LANDSCAPE

LANCASHIRE'S FAIR FACE

LANCASHIRE–WESTMORLAND HIGHWAY

THE CURIOUS TRAVELLER THROUGH LAKELAND

WEST PENNINE HIGHWAY

THE CURIOUS TRAVELLER: LANCASTER TO LAKELAND

LANCASHIRE COUNTRYGOER

COUNTRYGOER IN THE DALES

PORTRAIT OF LANCASHIRE

COUNTRYGOER'S NORTH

NORTH WALES FOR THE COUNTRYGOER

LANCASHIRE'S OLD FAMILIES

THE CURIOUS TRAVELLER THROUGH LAKELAND

Historic Ways North from Kendal and Cartmel to Keswick and Penrith

JESSICA LOFTHOUSE

Illustrations by the Author

ROBERT HALE & COMPANY

First edition 1954
Second edition 1973
Reprinted 1976

ISBN 0 7091 3489 4

Robert Hale & Company
Clerkenwell House
Clerkenwell Green
London EC1R 0HT

Printed and bound in Great Britain by
REDWOOD BURN LIMITED
Trowbridge & Esher

CONTENTS

SOME CURIOUS TRAVELLERS

LATE in the eighteenth century there first appeared in Lakeland strange creatures who, for lack of a better name, came to be known as "curious travellers". They travelled for travel's sake and enjoyed it, an entirely new thing in England, where men had previously travelled only when compelled. Some stayed to paint the mountains and lakes, some wrote elegant odes, some were just unashamed "rubber neckers", the first trickle of tourists which had by the turn of the century developed into a steady flow. After a century of pedestrian tourists, travellers in post-chaises and carriages, came a spate of eager "Lakers" carried hither in the "railroad coaches". They still come by rail, road and the modern motor-coach, a flood of travellers just as curious as the first to gaze upon the Lakeland scene, but with very different reactions. They no longer recoil from the "chaotic majesty and horrific splendour" of the mountains; I have heard of none who turned back out of overwhelming fear when faced by the Jaws of Borrowdale, or who quailed at the foot of the Sty or the Stake Pass as eighteenth-century visitors did. Yet they come for the same reasons given by Thomas West, whose *Guide to the Lakes* in 1770 was the first of many.

In West's time they came "to unbend the mind from anxious cares and fatiguing studies"—to be charmed by the "sights of sweet retreats and enchanting regions of calm repose". Said West, "Such as spend their lives in cities and their time in crowds will here meet objects that will enlarge the mind by contemplation." There is still a great deal of contemplation, standing and staring—and there always will be, away from the few highroads through the heart of the Lake country. We have more reason to seek the benefits West set out for the encouragement of eighteenth-century tourists.

Said Mr. Cumberland, the writer of *Ode to the Sun* in his dedication to George Romney, "In truth, a more pleasing tour than these lakes hold out to men of leisure and curiosity cannot be devised."

The first really curious traveller who wrote down in detail reactions during a Lakeland tour was a woman, a spinster in her thirties, who on a side-saddle, with spare mounts, with a companion and servant or two, came north to Westmorland by way of Preston, Lancaster and Kendal, in A.D. 1697. She came with no other motive than the satisfying of an insatiable curiosity and an urge to travel. At Mrs. Rowlandson's in Kendal she ate such delicious potted charr that she had to visit Lake Windermere, from which this delicacy came, travelling by narrow byways—probably by Staveley—where she noted that horse travel was the only method in local use, that carriages were impossible and that commodities when not carried in panniers on horses were taken in "little wheelbarrows drawn by horses". After taking boat to Belle Isle—noting the fish, the clarity of the lake-water, a weed she thought to be samphire, watching the making of oatcake, she journeyed along the lake until she came to the mountain road to Ullswater—probably Kirkstone Pass, so steep, it was unsafe to ride down the hills, and so rough and stony the roads tore off the horseshoes and wore them so thin she had to have them renewed. She came to a hamlet of "sad little huts" so primitive she thought the houses were merely "barns to fodder cattle in"—probably Hartsop or Patterdale. For refreshment she was offered clapbread, butter, cheese and a cup of beer.

This she considered poor fare—but found the local blacksmith's work on refurnishing her horse with shoes unbeaten in its excellence. Passing through Gowbarrow Park she noted "deer skipping about and haires"—and indulged in a little illicit coursing with a greyhound which accompanied her at this part of her travels. At the lower end of the lake, a green and gentle countryside, she noted that here she was leaving "those barren and rocky hills, not that they are limited to Westmorland only, for had I gone farther to the left hand on into Cumberland I should have found more such, and they tell me far worse for height and stonyness——". So to Penrith with its antiquities and fabulous giant stones, to Lowther Castle—before breakfast—and on to the north and Carlisle. A pity she did not probe farther into the Cumberland mountains; a most enterprising woman and emancipated well before the time. At a tea-party of immortals I would like to hear Celia Fiennes exchange experiences with others who came after—with Mrs. Radcliffe, who wrote of the horrors of the Lakeland scene with—I feel sure—her tongue in her cheek, Dorothy Wordsworth, Miss Weeton, Felicia Hemans, Harriet Martineau, Mrs. Lynn Linton—and maybe with Queen Adelaide and Queen Victoria, who did not write about the Lakes, but whose patronage led to a boom in Lake-ward travel.

A few years after Celia Fiennes came Daniel Defoe, commissioned to write his *Tour Through England and Wales.* Where he did not see the country for himself he wrote from hearsay and quoted from the works of others, notably the antiquary Camden, who had travelled into Cumberland and Westmorland in search of historic relics. One is rather suspicious about Defoe's actual travels into the Lakes. Soon after leaving Lancaster he allowed himself to exaggerate the mountain scene; the snow-capped heights reminded him of Merionethshire "and seemed to tell us that all the pleasant part of England was at an end". He was content to believe those who dilated upon the inhospitable terrors of the mountains and who insisted in "this barren, wild and frightful" region were only impassable mountains. Unlike Mrs. Fiennes he did not go to find out for himself if this were so. "Why dwell on the horrors?" he wrote, and set off from Kendal to Appleby, the "fruitful Eden valley", and so to Penrith and Carlisle. As far as the Lakes were concerned Defoe was lacking in curiosity.

In the mid-eighteenth century road improvement came. Carriage roads were opened out; along them came seekers after the romantic. In the first flow came one whose writings have hardly ever been excelled by any of his successors—Thomas Gray, the poet. In 1769 he set out with a companion, Dr. Warton, who was stricken with an attack of asthma at Brough and decided to leave his friend to continue alone to Lakeland. In his letters despatched at regular intervals to Dr. Warton is some of the best descriptive writing; in a few words he puts on paper the Lakeland scene in a way that we find fresh and delightful. Gray's approach from the north-east is rather unusual; most travellers came from Lancaster, over-sands, or from Kendal. His itinerary from Brough to Appleby and Penrith brought him into the Lakes by some of the best-known and best-loved routes, used to-day. He found Eamont-side paths to Dunmallet and Pooley Bridge, but unfortunately saw Ullswater only as far as Matterdale road end. He rejoiced in the beauty of the Derwentwater scene though after hearing tales of eagles and wild passes beyond Grange in Borrowdale he was not tempted to probe farther into that ancient kingdom "of Chaos and Old Night".

In Mr. Cumberland's ode came the oft-quoted lines describing the Lakeland mountains as "gigantic shapes" rearing their heads against the sky as if they—"Sons of Chaos and Primeval Night"—meant to war against it—stabbing at the heavens with their pointed and jagged peaks.

Leaving Keswick—on an enchanting October morning—Gray, looking from Castlerigg, was tempted to turn back again—not the first, nor the last, to feel so inclined. His route from there was over Naddle Fell to Thirlmere and lake to lake, Grasmere, Rydal, Windermere, to Kendal. Surely no traveller since has captured the spirit of Lakeland so well in so short a time.

A little later the first *Guide to the Lakes* was compiled by a most curious resident—Thomas West, a learned historian, writer of the *Antiquities of Furness*, who had lived at Sizergh, in the household of Stricklands, at Ulverston, and died at Sizergh Castle in 1779, being buried in Kendal church. His guide is valuable because it includes, as Addenda, the tour of Thomas Gray, as well as the works of other "esteemed writers", Arthur Young, Thomas Pennant and Dr. Brown, whose writings West consulted before he journeyed through the Lakes collecting information, as he said, "from local gentlemen".

From the 1770's travellers came north with West's Guide in their valises. From it they learned that nowhere else in so small a tract of country was there such variety of Alpine scenes—that every mountain was accessible to its summit and furnished prospects no less surprising and with more variety than the Alps themselves—that roads were good and the inns provided food "at present not excelled in any quarter of the empire". They took his advice—they provided themselves with telescopes "for viewing the fronts and summits of inaccessible rocks"—they carried, like Gray himself, landscape mirrors, that is "Plano-convex glasses to remove objects great and near to a due distance", substitutes for camera obscura "and obtainable from any optician". They followed his suggested routes, arriving over-sands from Lancaster with the Ulverston carriers or hired guides, or, the more timorous, by way of Kendal, where post-chaises could be obtained, or along the Cartmel coast from Leven Bridge and the Kent estuary. Thereafter, having arrived within the charmed circle of lakes and mountains they were quite willing to let him take them by the hand, or the bridle—to stop here or there as he bid them, to look east or west, up or down, to admire the beauty spots or enjoy the "elegant prospects" from detailed viewpoints. His book is a succession of Stations—the first a little above the village of Nibthwaite to gaze on Coniston Water, for Father West believed to enter Lakeland by this lake, to continue over High Cross to Esthwaite Water and Windermere "horse ferry" and from thence to travel north by Rydal, Grasmere and Thirlmere to Derwentwater, visiting Bassenthwaite Lake, Crummock Water and Buttermere in their turn, and Ullswater after a return to Keswick, was the ideal order. He blazed the trail and the seven, nine and eleven Lake Tours can do no better.

More "curious residents" wrote guides for curious travellers and visitors—Mr. Green of Ambleside wrote one, and William Wordsworth took a respite from poetry to compile his prose

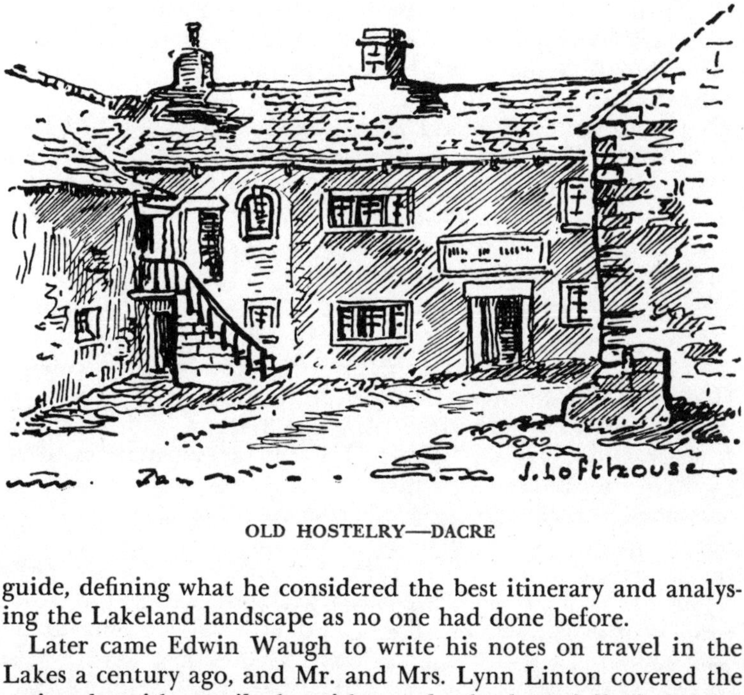

OLD HOSTELRY—DACRE

guide, defining what he considered the best itinerary and analysing the Lakeland landscape as no one had done before.

Later came Edwin Waugh to write his notes on travel in the Lakes a century ago, and Mr. and Mrs. Lynn Linton covered the region, he with pencil, she with note-book—both full of observations prompted by sheer curiosity. In neither of these books do the "horrors" come. The appreciation of the scene had changed in a hundred years. What had Dr. Dalton written in his elegant verse? This was the eighteenth-century attitude.

> "Horrors like these at first alarm,
> But soon with savage grandeur charm
> And raise to noblest thoughts the mind."

Many came, were delighted, impressed, invigorated, inspired. In what different ways did the Wordsworths and their friends, and Keats, Shelley, Ruskin, Rossetti react! Charles Lamb, somewhat against his will, succumbed to the beauty of Lakeland and became as ardent a " Laker " as any of his friends. And still they come—and each finds some aspect of the country to which he seems especially attuned. There are a thousand and one ways of seeing the Lake country and each is the best one. Everyone feels he has his own particular niche, his own sense of possession and belonging there.

This book is Lakeland seen through the eyes of many curious travellers who have recorded their delight in travelling through the dales from the seventeenth century onwards. It is also a personal itinerary of travel from Cartmel through the heart of Westmorland and Cumberland in the years 1949-51. The highways, modern, and those used by travellers on horseback, in post-chaise and carriage, in pre-turnpike and turnpike days, provide the framework for the book, but as I cannot resist the mountain tracks nor the fell paths there is considerable rambling and scrambling progress too.

Since I wrote this book and its follow-on, *The Curious Traveller : Lancaster to Lakeland,* my horizons have widened. Had these been written *after* the Alps, Norway and the Arctic, the unimaginable splendours of Arizona, Oregon and Utah, the Rockies and Colorado Canyon, I know my superlatives would have been restrained.

I have returned from such " big countries " my love of Lakeland undiminished. Nature here is not overlord as in the Rockies and the Canyon Country, where man, the puny creature, has hardly a look-in. I thank my lucky stars I was born British, and North-country at that, where one lifetime can allow one to come to love and know one's native land, not merely one small corner of it; where one can walk freely, and find paths to walk, as in the Lakes; where not to own a car is not the end of the world; where man and nature have worked long together and in centuries of so doing have created that " compact of beauty " called Lakeland.

I

LAKELAND APPROACHES—
HISTORIC AND ROMANTIC ROUTES

From Levens Park along the Kent to Kendal

From Kendal by Brigsteer woods, the Lyth valley and Winster to Windermere

The old coach road—Kendal—Crosthwaite—Gummers How to Newby Bridge

Ancient halls on the Kendal-Windermere Highway

Fell crossings—Kendal-Burneside, Hugill fells, Kentmere, Garburn Pass, Troutbeck, Skelgill, Windermere

Roadside Villages—Staveley and Ings

ROAD TOP—GUMMERS HOW

EASTERN APPROACHES

THE usual approach to the Lakes, by road—by car or bus, from Kendal to Windermere, is with slight variations the same travelled by tourists through the last two centuries. They caught their first glimpse of the lake from Alice How or Barker Knott, viewpoints on the two roads converging upon Bowness. In Wordsworth's 1822 Guide, his "Directions for the Tourist" gave the information that "much the greatest number of Lake tourists begin by passing from Kendal to Bowness; therefore our notices shall begin from that lake". So the poet-guide tells first of all the delights waiting by the Windermere shores. The Kendal-Staveley-Ings route was a favourite of Dorothy Wordsworth. Writing of the return from her brother's wedding, across Yorkshire, to Sedbergh and Kendal, Staveley she declared gave her most joy. She had happy memories of this "mountain village", and her first visit with William when they began "their pilgrimage together" in 1800. Coming along this road, the dale-head fells and mountains of the Kent valley seen afar are a magical sight. They have beckoned me away from the highroad more than once and, instead of dropping upon Windermere by the busy route of coaches and buses, I have come round about by way of Kentmere village, Garburn Pass, the Troutbeck valley and Jenkin Crag—much farther, but what a grand introduction to the beauty of the hills! I am all for the slow, meandering approach which gives one time to assimilate and savour the pleasures one by one.

Thomas West's guide concentrates on the approaches from the south, from the coast of Morecambe Bay, from Low Furness to High Furness, from Lowick and Coniston Water—and this to-day has much to commend it. I prefer to work updale from the estuaries, from the gentler scenes of Cartmel and Furness to the grandeur of the central massif. I find so much that is charming and unspoilt in the little valleys—along the Lyth from Gilpin Bridge, from Witherslack near Grange along the Winster river to Bowland Bridge, and northwards to Bowness, or by the Vale of Cartmel to Newby Bridge. Some of the old travellers rode the same routes with varying degrees of fear or apprehension. The coastal route advised by West as alternative to the sands crossing was from Levens Hall, along the Long Causeway to Beathwaite Green (along which now runs the straight highroad across the head of the Kent estuary), and from Witherslack over Towtop or Tautop—a most fearsome ascent up a corkscrew road, to Newton-in-Cartmel and Newby Bridge—this being the carriage road of the eighteenth century. For travel in greater comfort he advised the hiring of post-chaises at Kendal, from whence the route to Ulverston was uphill and down across a sequence of dales to Newby Bridge—"though mountainous and uneven, nevertheless in other respects it affords an agreeable ride". This was the exciting scenic highway which dropped from Gummers How to Fell Foot and the Windermere fords above Newby Bridge; using it, we travel behind a goodly company, and when we pause, entranced, at the top of Gummers How road we are only paying due tribute to a beauty that has arrested thousands before us. "You'll never get me to ride along such roads again," exclaimed a very nervous woman passenger, who stepped indignantly out of a car near this point. I was sketching the scene, the sentinel trees, the boulder walls, the enchanting glimpse of the blue bay below, and overheard what followed. "Such roads!" she grumbled, and took a few steps along the road. She stopped, gazed below and was silent. Turning to the driver, said she, "What roads! But, my—it was worth it." The Ulverston coaches came this way. How many passengers prayed fervently for a safe issue out of all their afflictions at this same point?

Before we start out on journeys through Lakeland proper, following in the footsteps of four centuries of curious travellers, let me tell of some very fine approaches across the fells near the Kendal highroad. One I shall never forget because I was actually returning homeward, rained off during one of the worst Easters I ever experienced; leaving Kendal, I was walking south along the fell road above Brigsteer when there came one of those nothing short of miraculous weather changes, when the sky opened, the sun burst forth, dazzling on snow-clad mountains and on clearings bright gold with wild daffodils. At once, I changed my direction, turned north, and was away to the Lakes, obeying a call which could not be denied. Another unorthodox entry was along the Kent river from Kendal, to Burneside, from farm to farm in the fells of Hugill, over lonely heights already coloured with the brush of autumn into the Kentmere valley and into the clouds above Garburn Pass to Troutbeck and Ambleside. A third most exciting journey was in the afternoon of a golden November day when, after crossing Shap Fell by bus, I took to my feet at Lowther village, passed through the Park to Askham and had to myself all the glories of sunset on the prehistory-haunted fell called Moor Divock which overlooks the lower reaches of Ullswater; Pooley Bridge was my goal that day. After these introductions I am sure I was better attuned to the "heart of Lakeland" scene than if I had started my walking from Bowness or Ambleside or Pooley Bridge.

In the same way, I enjoy Kendal best when I approach the old grey town by the older byways east of the present main road. There is a delightful walk few take, from the bridge at Levens, through the Park of Levens, where stand in avenues, in groups, in solitary beauty, some of the finest chestnuts, oaks, beeches in the north country.* In wild weather when the Kent river roars by and the tree-tops are tossed in the wind, there are strange pockets of stillness and silence in the shelter of these avenues. Long ago travellers collecting curiosities were most interested in local tales of the roaring of the Kent river falls. Celia Fiennes referred to this curiosity—"the roaring of the water at these places does sometime foretell wet weather, they do observe that when the water do roar most in the fall on the northside it will be faire, if on the southside it will be wet—the same observation is made at Lancaster." West did not mention this method of foretelling the weather, but he did advise his tourists returning south from their grand tour of the Lakes to ride down the east side of the Kent from Kendal to Levens Park—"If you are not supplied with

* The avenue was saved in 1970 by the re-siting of the Kendal by-pass.

the Key from Kendal, the Keeper must be applied to." He thought highly of this Park—" one of the sweetest spots that Fancy can imagine. The woods, the rocks, the river, the grounds, are rivals in beauty of style, and variety of contrast. . . . Thickets cover the brows; ancient thorns, and more ancient oaks, are scattered over the plain, and clumps, and solitary beech trees of enormous size, equal, if not surpass, anything the Chiltern Hills can boast. The Park is well stocked with fallow deer."

Much of West's description after almost two hundred years still holds good. No river is lovelier, looping in pools—sometimes turquoise blue, sometimes peacock green, under overhanging limestone scars, the haunt of herons and kingfishers. The deer have not been banished; one March morning I came unaware upon a number of them. They were as astonished as I, but stood their ground with admirable calm whilst I tried to merge with a moss-grown tree-trunk. The largest among them, a fine, handsome buck, kept them by his example in check, staring in my direction. There were a score of them, as brown as the trees themselves, four young bucks and the rest graceful little does. They milled about, gave little skips and jumps, the bucks playfully pushed and prodded, but not once did their watchful eyes leave me. This I observed near the look-out knoll which was once crowned by a summer-house, a favourite retiring-place for Bellingham ladies—Diana's Temple—a charming spot. At Archers Hill I left the Deer Park behind me, my way now following quiet sheltered lanes to Force Bridge, a place visited in the eighteenth century because of the falls and the forges. I found the Kent rushing through a deep, rock-walled ravine which had the ruined walls of Basing-ghyll Mill overlooking it. Upriver the gorge is spanned by a single-arched bridge of the pack-horse type, a dramatic and romantic spot. West, writing of this " singular romantic " scene, describes the bridge as of " unknown antiquity—of venerable appearance " but, said he, " the beauty of the stream is much impaired since the forge was erected ". Thomas Gray, curious to see the forge at work, came here " from the Millthrop turnpike near Sizergh "—this on his return from his tour of the Lakes and during his stay at Kendal. He wrote, " The calmness and brightness of the evening, the roar of the waters, and the thumping of huge hammers at the iron forge not far distant made it a singular walk. . . . I walked down to the forge and saw the demons at work by the light of their own fires. The iron is brought in pigs to Millthrop by sea from Scotland——." Iron forges were a common sight in and around the fringe of Lakeland two centuries ago, wherever wood was available for fuel for the smelting.

Wandering around I found banks of wild violets—white and delicately scented—near the wood called Pigwilly. Purple primulas bloomed by cottage walls in the tiny community grouped near the ford where Nanny Pie Lane crosses the Kent for Sedgwick village. Near here, scattered in copses, are relics of a derelict gunpowder works, clothed by the healing hand of Nature and Time. All is untouched countryside following the river northwards, green, gentle and overlaid by the cultivation of long centuries. Not far away pleasant lanes link Sedgwick with Natland and Kendal and sometimes the whistle of the Royal Scot comes on the wind; from the old canal comes no sound and anyone choosing to follow the towpath to Kendal will have only his own thoughts for company. I chose the river bank to Hawes Bridge—two arches flung over rocky channels and flat, stone-slab tables which make one think at once of summer days and picnics by the river—after which Hawes Lane took me to the canal, a half-dry watercut with grass-grown towpath. No traffic-dodging problems here; uninterrupted progress and the distant prospect of Kendal, and historic sites left and right: a Roman candlestick was found near the third bridge in 1903; the Roman camp at Watercrook in a horseshoe bend of the Kent; on Helm Fell a Roman signal station at Castlesteads, which, as West wrote, communicated with forts north and south "by smoke in the day, by flame in the night". But now we cannot ignore the motorway.

KENDAL—OLD AND NEW

Entering by the canal way is an introduction to industrial Kendal. Ancient and historic the place is, yet always strangers have commented on its activities in mart and manufactory. Celia Fiennes in the late seventeenth century commented on its famous "cottons"—which were of course woollens—and were used for blankets and for the Scots' plaids. "There is much made here and also linsiwoolseys and a great deal of leather tanned here and all sorts of commodities", and to its markets came "abundance of horses . . . with their burdens". Defoe mentioned the prevalence of woollen manufacture, and Thomas Gray approaching in the evening from Staveley noted the many tenter grounds which he at first mistook for houses, and were indeed open spaces where cloth was spread out by the weavers.

Even West with his predilection for antiquities wrote: "The objects most worthy of notice here are the manufactures . . . Kendal cottons, a coarse woollen cloth, of linseys and knit worsted stockings . . . a considerable tannery . . . lesser manufactures of fish hooks, of waste silk which is received from London and after scouring, combing and spinning is returned, and wool cards. . . . Other industries worth seeing are mills for scouring, fulling, and sizing cloth, for cutting and rasping dying wood, etc. . . ." West drew the attention of strangers to the flourishing state of Kendal trade due to the industry of its people, reminding them of the fillip which the laws of Richard the Second and Henry the Fourth gave to the making of Kendal Cottons.

Entering the town now by the great K shoe factory—and wandering along Kent side, into the busy yards and alleys, noting the great variety of industries, large and small, we realize that at no time in history has Kendal stood still. Unlike many towns in the north it never put all its industrial eggs in one basket so its inhabitants have never been distressed by the worst unemployment problems and trade slumps.

Tourists to-day miss the best of Kendal if they merely visit the parish church and the castle ruins; the chief delights are again various and scattered throughout the long main highway and side-streets—which are called "gates". The yards should be explored in turn or as whim directs, strangers should talk to the old folk who loiter near the archways which give entry to their hidden homes, and from overlooking heights the more curious of the travellers should watch the play of light and shade, sun and cloud, over the chimneys and roof-tops. The poet in Thomas Gray saw Kendal from the castle hill "as if the houses had been dancing a country dance and were out; there they stand back to back, corner to corner, some uphill, some down, without intent or meaning". To-day we can see the intent; Kendal grew up between the Nether Bridge and Stramogate Bridge, along the highroad to Penrith by Shap, along the highway climbing by the House of Correction Hill to Bowness and Ambleside, up Beast Banks, along the road linking Kendal with Newby Bridge and Ulverston. Where these old routes met the town grew up; from numerous breaches in the old streets branched the yards, each housing distinct communities with cottages, inns, workshops, each one of which possessed a gateway or barrier to keep out undesirables. Often the undesirables must have been Scots raiders who swept through Kendal too frequently in the Middle Ages. On the west side of the main north-south street the yards peter out at the foot of a steep hillside; on the east side the yards run down to the river. But many were demolished in the 1960's.

During my walk up the Kent from Levens Bridge the weather had been wild and windy but not wet. My arrival at Kendal coincided with a storm which drove me into the church from the pelting rain in Kirkland. The wide naves were dim as twilight, the colours of the stained glass windows darkened. An invisible organist played sombre music upon an invisible organ. No one stirred until I was conscious of two girls, in school uniform of Kendal green, tiptoeing down an aisle. We joined forces. "We've got to find Robin the Devil's cap, Katharine Parr's uncle's tomb, a pillar with four claws carved at its base and a vicar's memorial which begins 'London bred me, Westminster fed me'."

The last we found first. I had already made a copy of the quaint epitaph, written for himself by Mr. Tyrer in 1627.

"London bred mee, Westminster fed mee,
Cambridge sped mee, my sister wed mee,
Study taught mee, Living sought me,
Learning brought mee, Kendal caught me,
Labour pressed me, Sickness distressed me,
Deathe oppressed me, the Grave possessed mee,
God first gave mee, Christ did save mee,
Earth did crave mee, and Heaven would have me."

The girls tracked down all they required and found much else besides. The storm passed, light grew and we saw the beauty of the Easter decorations—the delicate wild daffodils "that take the winds of March with beauty", golden sprays of forsythia, primroses cushioned in green mosses, damson blossom on the ledges. Spring had arrived in Westmorland.

ROUNDABOUT—KENDAL, TO LYTH AND WINSTER VALLEYS, AND WINDERMERE

The next two days were of a wildness unsurpassed. I rambled around Kendal, sought shelter in archways when the worst rainstorms swept over and concentrated when outdoor occupation was impossible on the interiors of the many ancient buildings within the town. I met many walkers, but all were going south, rained off, driven homeward by gales, snowstorms and bitter cold. On the third morning I also turned south, regretfully. Rain had prevented my finishing drawings of Collinfield, the fine old manor house of the Sedgwicks which has given its name to one of Kendal's modern housing estates and is hidden away behind avenues of semi-detached houses. At one time, during the seventeenth century, when the grandson of the builder, Jeffrey Sedgwick, was private secretary of the Lady Anne Clifford, that much-travelled lady was often guest here, discussing business connected with her various Westmorland estates. The house has seen better days; now Collinfield is a farm with barnyard fowl and many waddling ducks about the place. I did what I could of my sketch and turned away in the rain on the highroad as far as Helsington Laithes. At this neighbouring manor house, which lies a short distance from A6 and faces the road, are architectural features older than those at Collinfield, parts dating from the fifteenth century when the Bindlosses — a family associated with Borwick Hall farther south—owned it, and from the sixteenth, when the Bellinghams of Levens Hall added wings and out-buildings. It is quite charming, even in heavy rain, and an attractive track passes its northern walls, climbing to the high level lane along the scar top to Brigsteer. I was rained off, like all the other Easter walkers, but I was determined to enjoy the country on my way to Levens Bridge.

COLLINFIELD—KENDAL

From this high-level byway there are distant views towards the higher Westmorland fells and mountains as enchanting as those which greet the traveller from the scar top above Cunswick Hall and Underbarrow. The Scots can sing as long as they wish how the " far Coolins are pulling me away ", but for sheer compelling invitation give me the Lakeland scene from these heights. I turned south, but despite hailstones, black clouds, fierce winds, my longing was for the north. Each time I looked backwards the landscape seemed more magical. And at noon, standing high on the brow above little Brigsteer, listening, and watching the wind's play in the green larches and in the bent spruces on the brown fell, looking down to the dale floor where men worked in a ploughed field and all seemed to be a flat calm, I saw one gleam of hope. Southwards over Morecambe Bay rays of sunlight parted the clouds and above the shoreline villages was just one patch of blue sky. A minute later I had my first undoubted rendezvous with spring. Kestrels were hovering above the fell and crows clamouring over rocky ledges, but within a copse of hazel, oak and holly called Honeybee Wood, I entered a silent haven, full of delicious green wood scents; I found a little hollow where primroses grew in damp cushions and the woodland floor was covered with " bedded violets that fill March woods with dusky passion "; they were everywhere carpeting the ground with purple. Wandering on I came into a neighbouring clearing; here it was I saw the happiest sight of the morning: hundreds of dancing daffodils—the wild daffodils of poetry with which the heavy stiff-stemmed, bright yellow garden variety bear no comparison. As I picked a bunch of them birds carolled on every side, a squirrel came out to peep, a light rain swept across the flowers, the sun burst forth. I looked up, expecting to see a rainbow—and there it was arching over the Lyth valley, trembling over white-walled farms, over orchards blossoming white with damson blow, over crofts gold with daffodils. Beyond the rainbow was a beauty and an invitation which could not be gainsaid —mountains white with snow, fells purple and gold in the sun— the Enchanted Land.

I did not continue south. I turned north towards those delectable mountains and did not think of home-going until three days later. In Lakeland such wizard transformations are not uncommon. After the most lowering, glowering sulks, the weather suddenly changes mood and is most bewitching.

My way to Windermere was from Brigsteer village—where lanes come in from Levens Bridge and Levens village, on to

Tullathwaite and Underbarrow Beck, through the Lyth pastures—"Lythe" is a Norse name given to a hill slope—through the cheerful village of Crosthwaite where little children and early lambs ran races over hillocks covered with wild daffodils, and later along the Winster valley which is shared by Westmorland and Lancashire, a damson valley hung in snowy blossom. No approach to Windermere is more charming than this; comely farms of great age lie alongside the road, colourful copses clothe the slopes and reach down to the little Winster river. Many memories of earlier travellers linger hereabouts; around the valley are farms where the families in 1652 became "convinct" on hearing George Fox during his first great journey through the north-west. At the Underbarrow home of Miles Bateman he met the local "priest" and professors, winning over many local folk. One he "convinct" in 1652 was Miles Halstead of Mountjoy, Underbarrow, who became an earnest preacher all over the British Isles. His wife once complained sadly, "Would to God I had married a drunkard. Then I might have found him in the alehouse, but now I cannot tell where to find my husband."

The Winster by-roads meet the east-west routes from Kendal and Crook to the Windermere Ferry, this being the route by which the student William Wordsworth returned during holidays from university, savouring on this last lap all the joys of anticipation. The first glimpse of the lake is always a joyful sight—in summer with white swans and white-sailed yachts riding the bosom of the mirror-like water, or in early spring when there is a mist of green on the larches over the lake and bridal whiteness over the wild cherry trees on Claife Heights.

WAYS TO WINDERMERE

There are three road approaches to Windermere lake. Kendal, Crosthwaite Green, Bowland Bridge, Gummers How to Newby Bridge I have mentioned already as the busy eighteenth-century carriage road, an uphill and down switchback road with superb views from the crest of each hill. The Kendal to Crook and Windermere Ferry road is the next northwards, forking over a mile out of Kendal by a picturesque toll house possessing outsize cylindrical chimneys. It branches from A591, the Kendal-Windermere road, where improvements have spoilt some wayside landmarks but blasting through bedrock revealed splendid geological convolutions near Tolston Hall. Along each road there is something worth seeing, but most travellers are so eager to reach the lakes they have not time nor the inclination to go off the beaten track to discover what lies left and right. Hardly one of the neat farms scattered about the pastures, on the fell slopes or at the lane edge, but has some treasure. Most farms are seventeenth or early eighteenth century, as dated stones over porches or finely carved spice cupboards and court cupboards tell. The *Antiquities of Westmorland* includes scores of these farms in lists of houses containing interior woodwork of interest; Bradleyfield, Tranthwaite, Hag, Birks, Underhill, Fallen Yew, the Punch Bowl Inn and Broadoak lie near the Kendal-Crosthwaite road; Michelland, High Cleabarrow, Lindeth, Bellman Ground and Bellman Houses are near the Winster-Crook lane, and Crook End, High Leys, Sunnybrow, Field Tenement, and Sanderhill are farms near Crook. Then there is Crook Low Fold, and Ashes farm on the by-road to Staveley, and Hollins Hall, near Staveley, which has developed in stages from a fourteenth-century pele built over a stone-vaulted basement. These are but a few. Older still and with the antiquity more obvious to a stranger are two fine halls, both homes of families important in the history of the Kendal Barony—Burneside Hall, lying a mile to the east of the Kendal-Staveley road, near the River Kent, and Cunswick Hall sheltered by high scars which run between the Kendal-Crosthwaite and Kendal-Crook roads.

Cunswick Hall the curious traveller *must* see. The lane—a rough farm track—begins just beyond the second milestone from Kendal on the Crook road, a delightful way beginning as a narrow enclosed lane and beyond the only gate entering open pastures where in spring the sky is filled with the bubbling cries of curlews and, likely enough, a hare stands surveying the landscape with appreciative eye. I once startled Malkin and he went lolloping ahead of me, stopping when I stopped, until finally he turned into the intakes near the tiny green tarn which is so beautifully framed at the foot of Cunswick Scar. Here prehistoric people had a camp on rising ground, but there is nothing to see, only "grey wether" boulders scattered around after the Ice Age.

Along the top of the limestone scars, white cliffs with black yews gripped in crevices, it is said there walks the ghost of one of the Leyburnes. The Leyburnes of old were a desperate, belligerent lot and many wild deeds were enacted upon their land. To-day it is a very peaceful spot, a mile removed from roads and highways, linked only with neighbours by rough tracks such as the one we are on. When men first lived here their strong pele was defence against raiding Scots; only the gateway with its spy holes and arrow slits remains, a fifteenth-century outer defence with arches, later rebuilt and the proud arms of the Tudors inset therein. Tradition asserts that here came Henry VIII to woo the young widow, Katharine Parr, and romance has it that the king pressed his suit in the yew walk. Some of the yews remain. Maybe from local-grown yews Sir James Leyburne furnished his twenty retainers with bows when they rode forth with him to the great muster against the Scots in 1544. Their womenfolk must have climbed the scar to watch the last of the men as they rode away to the north—and when news came that the Leyburnes were

BURNESIDE HALL

home returning they must again have climbed to the scar top to wait for them. A far-flung view, one which holds all the best of Westmorland in it, unrolls itself to the west.

Burneside Hall has retained more of its ancient defences than Cunswick. It is one of the best old peles to be seen in the north-west, having its stone tower—a ruin, but showing its original form—an almost complete high wall surrounding an enclosure into which animals were driven for safety, and a fine gatehouse with a venerable door still preserved in the archway. A section of a wide moat with stone causeway is there too—as though its sole function is to reflect the fine buildings within its surface. Soon after the Conquest, when this part of the Barony of Kendal was called Stirkland—from the large quantities of young stock raised in the district—Brunolfshede was "on the map". The land of one Roger of Brunolfshede became the Manor of Strickland, whereas land farther south owned by Uchtred, son of Ketel, became and is still known as Strickland Ketel. In the thirteenth century an heiress of Burneside called Elizabeth married John Wessington from Durham—through whom the Washingtons came to own lands around Crook and Strickland Ketel and also around Carnforth and Tewitfield. Later, marriage of an heiress brought the Bellinghams to Burneside and a sixteenth-century addition of theirs was the hall built south of the pele, which no longer appeared an attractive dwelling. This has become the present farmhouse.

Burneside Hall is on the outskirts of Burneside village, which is two miles from Kendal on the by-road along the Kent valley. Lanes fork right to Burneside from the Kendal-Windermere road and one between an avenue of superb beeches is excuse in itself for the stranger to make a diversion. The village has grown up by roaring falls which over a century ago decided the site for the well-known paper mills. An unusual village, its cottages and rows of houses have an architecture and planning of their own. I have seen no place quite like it.

When Cropper and Co. started paper making at Burneside and Cowan Head mills their output in the first year was a modest 250 tons. In 1950 they produced 16,650 tons of wrapping paper at the Kent-side mills. The village reflects this prosperity.

The Hall stands in its own quiet acres among trees and backed by rounded green hills; the land wears the appearance of having been cared for continuously for centuries. Nothing is waste or poor land, but all is rich and green and a delight to the eye. My sketch shows the western side of the hall; the eastern range is equally interesting. I made the drawing on a windy day when cat's-paws were stroking the shallow waters of the pond, the wind was blowing vigorously in the mantle of creepers around the pele and young lambs huddled by their mothers in the small shelter of tree roots. It was not the kind of day to bring Burneside babies in their prams to watch the "chuckies" at the farm and the "quack-quacks" on the pond, nor for the old pensioners to take their ease and put the world to rights as they sit on the wayside seat at the cross-roads. But it was the day for brisk walking along the lane which hugs the fell foot for three miles to Staveley. Little traffic comes this way though the surface is good and the landscape charming. Anyone wishing to take a preview of Westmorland fell country might well turn off along any of the farm tracks branching from this lane and very soon he will consider the busy outer world well lost. How many lovers of Lakeland know of the lonely tracks from Godmund Hall and Hundhow which come to Side House, a little farm tucked away between bracken-covered slopes and a rocky gill full of noisy waterfalls, or of Brundknott which stands by the same linking grass-floored lane, or realize the nook-shotten charm of the tiny valleys which cut into the fells of Hugill?

This was our approach to Windermere one September day, one quite memorable for its golden sunshine and the colourful tapestry of the landscape. We followed the Kent out of Kendal, to Burneside Hall and along the Staveley lane as far as Godmund

BARMKYN WALL—BURNESIDE HALL

Hall where we turned along the fell-edge tracks, discovering parts of Westmorland rarely heard of though they are so near highways. We came over high ridges to the Kentmere valley where we stayed the night, then over higher fells to Troutbeck and the Windermere country the following morning. Such an approach I commend to any wanderer in no particular hurry "to get there". There is nothing which is not fair to look upon—nothing aggressively modern, unless it be the diatomite works in the lower part of Kentmere, and nothing to disturb a peace which must have wrapped Over Staveley and Hugill since they were given these names.

It is not a thickly peopled region—nook-shotten describes it well. The prettiest white-walled farms are dotted upon the fell-sides or grip the high banks of cascading becks near the dale floors. Through open doors you see the soft gleam of oak rafters, a court cupboard elaborately carved, a spice cupboard with a seventeenth-century date. You meet the countryfolk, a man scything brackens, a boy whistling to a sheep-dog invisible to us on a high knott, children playing by farm doors.

But when you come into Elfhow-lane—surely named from a fairy mound—and take to the fell beyond Park House, the highest farm, you see no one, see no sign of humankind. This is the high way to Kentmere, loveliest when autumn has yellowed the bents and the heather smoulders with dying crimson. The path is narrow, across boggy places scented heavily with bog myrtle, over slopes where the juniper bushes and hollies are dark shapes against the rust-red brackens. All around us is silent—the curlews have gone—until the winds come sweeping over the heights from Longsleddale or over the craggy tops from Mardale.

Many tiny becks are cradled here; when they begin their descent to the dale of the Kent they make tinkling music, like small children singing to themselves for company. In the walled intakes at lower level are village sites, cattle pens and sheep folds of pre-Roman Celts.

Our way, marked on maps as a bridle path, joins the road near Long Houses—a long range of eighteenth-century farm buildings—only three miles direct from Staveley village. So near the busy highway of motor-coach tours and streams of cars yet a world away in quietness.

The Kent once ran out of its high mountains into a flat dale bottom which had been most effectively dammed by the debris of glacial moraine. Here the Kent Mere spread across the valley floor, a place for fish and water fowl until, less than a century ago, the natural dam was partly breached and the water began to drain away. I have met old people who told of the mere of their youth, where fishing was still possible and lads could skate in hard frost. Then came the complete draining of the lake and the discovery of thick deposits of clay containing diatoms just beneath the overlying beds of peat. And the number of uses to which this diatomite clay can be put is surprising. We use it in face powder—and in metal polish; it gives an egg-shell finish to paints and goes into the making of paper, rubber, plastic and floor-coverings; it is used in almost everything which is insulated against heat and cold and in eliminating sound, and where containers for chemicals are manufactured, and in filtering liquids of all kinds—there diatomite clay has its use also. As the clay in the old mere bed is more than twenty feet in depth and extends over 150 acres the supplies should keep industry going for a long time to come.

From the fell we saw little sign of the works and at Long Houses we were beyond the old lake levels.

Our way took us updale to a farm perched high on a steep slope, like a knot it looked in a tangle of grey walls. First the lane ran downhill to New Bridge with the Kent, clear as crystal, chuckling over grey pebbles. The house near by (marked Temp. Hotel on maps to delude strangers, for it does not cater for wayfarers) was once an inn, and the subject of a fiercely fought lawsuit (Sharp *v.* Wakefield) in the House of Lords. Kentmere Inn made legal history as the first to lose its licence for allowing heavy drinking and immorality under its roof. Before it fell on bad days it had been the meeting-place for convivial evenings enjoyed by shepherds and farmers of three dales—Troutbeck, Sleddale and Kentmere; three roads met here.

"Once on a dark, misty night I had a scare along this lane," said a farmer, solemnly. "Couldn't see my hand in front of me. Then behind me—footsteps following. I stopped—they stopped. I went on—they went on. 'Who are you?' I shouted. No answer. My hair lifted on my head wi' fright. The steps hurried past. I stopped. I tried to strike a match but my hands trembled too much. Then I got a light and peered all around me. I saw two green eyes staring back. It was only a little three-legged Herdwick after all!"

Evening draws in early, after a lavish spell of sunset's flame and gold over the craggy sky-line on Garburn. Sad, cold winds sweep down from the great mountains which divide us from Mardale. A great silence falls, broken only by the coughing of an old ewe, bleating of lambs, and from a borran, one of the tumbled piles of boulders which have been there since the glaciers retreated, came the bark of a fox.

"Foxes," says the farmer as we all sit round the fire in the lamplight, "we've been overrun with the vermin. May's our worst month for losses in lambs. Myself, I never follow the hunt, but I get a grand-stand view from the farmyard. I reckon I've been in at the kill ahead of many a follower."

I mentioned the blood-curdling scream I had once heard out of the mountain mists up Kentmere.

"That wouldn't be Reynard but a hound. You know, hunting as we do it gives fox a humane death. He runs to earth, terrier goes in after him, and seizes hold. Huntsman pulls terrier out, then catches fox by his brush, throws him to the hounds. There's a pounce and all is over. Cleaner death than a bad shot."

Behind the farm is a high crag "teeming wi' foxes". Joe Bowman, a huntsman famous as John Peel in these parts, once found himself stuck for words, a rare occurrence, for he was known for his rich flow of language. On Cover Crag a fox had disappeared in a borran, a terrier streaked after him—and out ran not one but five foxes, so swiftly that Joe was dumbfounded.

We talked of field names, for each compartment of the maze of intakes, however small, has its name. Above Kentmere church are Hodgeon Close, Robin Green, Brow and Trinket, Back Wife, Butting Hall, Rook How and Jumb Paddock (with a Kent cascade roaring near by), Jane Meadow, Jossy Wife Field, and Bell, a field where long ago a bell was rung from a rock to warn the good folk that there was to be a service in the old church on the hill. We talked of storms, waterbursts, or gill brasts as they are called in Cumbria, and of one which tore down the slopes from Graven Gate to Hollow Bank and Overend.

From unwanted waters we turned to the fascinating subject of water divining. Dowsers had several times located underground springs on the farm. One was a furnace stoker in a steel works who came during haytime for outdoor work and at the same time acted as dowser.

"He used a willow wand. It wriggled and twisted on his fingers as he passed over water, then it leapt into the air. 'Bore down twelve feet,' he said. His arms looked withered. He rested and massaged them. Dowsing drains something out of a man." Another diviner known in these parts is a paper-worker from Burneside Mills; he uses hazel twigs. We had never thought of water shortages in Kentmere, a dale of becks and clear fountains, but as the farmer told us, "With a cow drinking ten gallons at a go, farms need well-filled troughs."

The next morning light grew out of an enveloping white mist which did not begin to dispel until we were on the way to Garburn Pass. Above the huddled farms of Kentmere the stony track climbs steeply to the fell, turning by a grey boulder-built barn. Everything about this country is primitive in its architecture, but the builder knew what style best suited material and local conditions. As the mist lifted we could see the rock-strewn slopes, the dark group of buildings at Kentmere Hall. Here the Gilpins of the fifteenth century built their pele as security against raiders. Stories associated with the hall include that of the "gurt lad", Hugh Hird, who was so strong he lifted one of the heavy oak beams into place, single-handed. He should be classed with the early travellers who saw beyond the limits of their native Westmorland. His strength was talked of beyond Kentmere and Troutbeck after his visit to the court of King Edward the Sixth, where he was bidden to show southerners how a lad of Westmorland could wrestle. Another traveller from Kentmere was the learned Tudor divine, Bernard Gilpin, who was known as the Apostle of the North, an early Protestant reformer who set out one sad day to face a martyr's death at the stake in London. On his way an accident delayed him; before he was fit to be moved Queen Mary was dead and so his life was saved. His brother, too, travelled far, as ambassador to the court of Holland.

The track climbs and coils, through heather and bracken, across chuckling becks, into green intermont hollows full of quietness. The mist lifts and we see that rowans are red-berried by rocky gills and crows fly about high crags on the sky-line. The sun catches up with us and shines upon the dale behind us, but, when we come at last to the head of the pass and look upon the Troutbeck valley, mist lies therein and wind brings a scattering of rain. There is mystery there, beauty to be guessed at. I know that Troutbeck Park fills the dale below and the beck threads the floor between tree-edged fields. I can imagine the pretty farms and cottages lined up on the far side of the dale and the grey road linking them which runs off to the dale head to enter the high pass of Kirkstone. A boggy pass ahead, a stony road to the village—but given a day with good visibility and there is no better way for feeling at the heart of things. We have not yet reached the lakes, our goal, but the spirit of the high hills is here.

More of this Troutbeck scene comes later in the book. For the walker bound for Windermere Lake there are downhill lanes from Troutbeck village and, better still, the walled-in and grass-floored lanes to High Skelgill Farm which loop the foot of Wansfell and have all the way superb views of the lake. These prospects seem to have been ignored by the eighteenth-century experts. West must not have heard of Jenkin Crag or I am sure he would have been up there detailing the charms of the landscape from this "station". Victorian guides had discovered it and in a battered copy of an eighty-year-old guide to Ambleside in my possession is included a folding panorama, "by the aid of which thirty-seven eminences can be easily recognized". The guide is full of observances. The brow of the precipice was "somewhat disfigured owing to vegetation and earth having caught fire during the celebration week of Victoria's Jubilee". A feature viewers should note is " the way the promontories of one shore of Windermere correspond with the bays of the opposite shore " as if they could be dovetailed with remarkable exactness if drawn together. And there are tales too of the gentleman highwayman, Monkswell, who hid his loot in Skelgill stables.

APPROACH FROM KENDAL

Now for the most used approach to Windermere which passes through the villages of Staveley and Ings, both places of great age. The road is not without beauty in both near and far views, there is infinite variety on either hand. I remember a June journey a year ago when I shared the front seat of a red Ambleside-bound bus with two Canadian women. " Could anything be lovelier than this? " they asked. I told them to wait. Yet the roadside scene was quite enchanting, for beyond the Burneside lane where the highway crosses Rather Heath the ground was misted with bluebells; or clad in gorse bushes bright as new-minted gold. When we passed through tree shade and looked upwards we saw deep blue —not the sky but fell slopes carpeted with bluebells; when we looked downwards into woodland clearings what we thought to be blue pools of water were indeed acres of bluebells. Beeches were in perfect clear green leafage and both oaks and ashes stood in loveliness against hyacinthine blue.

The seasons change, the colours flame and fade away, but the old houses are always there, and Staveley is ready to refresh the wayfarer, and the chapel door at Ings is open—just as it was when the Wordsworths came by. Staveley began existence as " the place where staves are grown "; it still concerns itself with wood and saw mills. We pass the seventeenth-century Stock Bridge Inn, the road runs alongside the Kent, passes the Duke William and the Eagle and Child—the village, being pre-eminently a wayside village catering for wayfarers, has its quota of inns—we notice the detached tower of the church, and catch sight of the Bobbin Mills with high stacks of logs adjacent. For generations Brockbanks have been wood turning here by the little River Gowan—turning bobbins of all kinds, door knobs and tool handles.

Staveley once woke up and played a part in Lakeland history —the period early in the reign of James I when that Scottish Solomon tried to tamper with old custom. For centuries Lakeland farmers had held their land by " border tenure ", a form of holding " estates " which began in the early days of border warfare. Because of the difficulties besetting all tenant farmers who lived south of the Scottish border, through whose valleys ran Scots raiding routes, they were granted special privileges in return for their valuable aid in helping to prevent, hinder, hold up or repel the enemy. The statesmen were a fine race of Cumbrians, proud, independent, and sticklers for their rights.

When the King's plan to abolish border tenure was made known, they chose Staveley as meeting-place to discuss ways and means of opposing him. Think of them, converging down all the long dales, striding along all the high ridges we can see from the highroad, out of Borrowdale, Bannisdale and Longsleddale, from Mardale over Nan Bield Pass to Kentmere, from Patterdale and Matterdale by Kirkstone, from the north along High Street and Garburn Pass, and tramping with heads held high and stern resolve in their hearts to the place of meeting. Some fine speeches must have been heard. And the statesmen got their way. James was prevailed upon to leave things as they were, though the Cumbrian farmers were not likely to be needed as a first line of defence any more.

Ings is two miles nearer Windermere, a scattered village which hides its older buildings out of sight of the highway. Old-world Ings is out of reach of wheels, in a little hollow watered by a merry beck on the right of the road. There white-haired old ladies stand at the doors of Robert Bateman's Almshouses. Down by the highway small children of Ings School hear the true life-story of the benefactor of their school, Robert Bateman, and on Sunday, at the chapel rebuilt with Robert Bateman's bequest, they see more written evidence to prove that what "teacher told them" is true.

In 1802 when Dorothy Wordsworth entered the chapel she saw it as "a neat little place with a marble floor and marble communion table—the marble had been sent by 'Richard' Bateman from Leghorn". Later William Wordsworth wrote the story of Bateman in verse—and there I read it on the north wall of the chancel. Who was this lad Bateman whose story is more vivid than that of Dick Whittington to Westmorland folk?

"He was a parish boy. At the church door
They made a gathering for him,
Shillings, pence and halfpence,
Wherewith the neighbours bought a basket
Which they filled with pedlar's wares.
With this basket went up the lad to London——"

So begins the tale of the local lad whose parents, unable or unwilling to help him, caused him to enlist the sympathy and generosity of the people of Ings. In London he tried his fortune. He was so faithful in a humble position in the household of a city merchant that he was advanced to the counting house and later sent to Italy to manage the Leghorn branch of his master's business. He earned a partnership and on the death of the benefactor became sole proprietor. He amassed great wealth and longed for the time when he could return home to Westmorland. He decided to build a house. Reston House, half-way between Staveley and Ings, was to be his home. But Fate decided he should never live there. In 1743 he made a will leaving £1,000 to buy land for the poor folk of Ings, to help in the upkeep of the village school which was then a century old. He left money for rebuilding the church and, for its greater adornment, transhipped Italian marble for the floors. Then he embarked in one of his own ships. But his captain was a villain whose plan to poison Bateman and appropriate the ship and cargo for himself succeeded. The body was thrown overboard in the Straits of Gibraltar. The captain turned back to Italy—and disappeared.

And that in brief is the tale of the local lad who made good and never forgot to be grateful to Ings which gave him the chance to do so. In turn Ings remembers him in gratitude. The chapel is small, dignified; the Italian marble is placed where Bateman intended.*

A mile onwards the road begins the last up and down stretch to Windermere Station, by Bannerigg and Alice How. This road offers their first glimpse of the Lake Country to possibly ninety-nine out of every hundred modern tourists. To many this is The Lakes. "Oh," they say, "I know the lakes. I once had a day at Windermere." As with the two Canadian women who cried "Can anything be more lovely?", seeing their first picture of beauty they are content to stay here. They are not in the curious traveller class.

Curious travellers today, like their predecessors of this book, are restless beings who never linger long in one place, rarely delay at the tourist meccas of Bowness and Ambleside; nor are they seen on A591. The rough and dangerous ways of the first lakers are now upgraded dual carriageway roads, so the wanderers of today are forced to the unspoilt walkers' paths, surprising solitudes

* Crime at sea? Bateman signed his will at Leghorn three days before his death in December 1743. There he is buried.

which no committed motorist—unless he forgets wheels whilst in Lakeland—can ever know.

These approach roads show clearly the pattern of tourism since the 60's. The upgraded Kendal-Windermere road enables thousands released from the Motorway to converge with greater ease and speed on Lakeland, persuaded to the " promised land " so that fears of resulting thrombosis ahead came into being. Broad dual carriageways forge relentlessly from Windermere to Keswick, shoving back the fells and cowing the mountain gods—so it seems.

After A591—my " Most Beautiful Road "—became a trunk road (tourism had to be served and commerce given free flow to the West Cumberland coast) the next threat was to A66. Was this east-west route across Lakeland from the Motorway and Penrith to Keswick and the industrial coast to become a trunk road south of the Skiddaw massif, or a new highway eating less ferociously into the Lakes to the north of it?

Lakeland is so small, so vulnerable. A new breed of tourist comes here, having seen the wonders of the world and loving this for its gentle, humanised, poetic beauty. More and more they converge upon it, turn from the overthronged A591 and A66 to the quiet valleys where they hope the old spirit of the Lakes is unchanged.

Again, the committed car-user destroys what he searches for. Summer weekends in the two Langdales, Borrowdale and even in remoter Wasdale and Ennerdale, and the lakeless Duddon and Eskdale, see such a congestion of cars that one envisages a time when " DALE FULL " notices must be put up in every cul-de-sac valley. Maybe, as in Derbyshire, a time will come when over-popular dales will be restricted—" PARK YOUR CAR HERE. MINIBUS SERVICE ONLY BEYOND THIS POINT ".

Curious travellers on foot have the freedom of the fell tracks and many miles of newly created paths for their sole pleasure. The curious walker is not the potential danger of the too curious motorist. And he has the best of it.

II

COASTWISE APPROACHES

From Levens Bridge to Witherslack

The Winster valley byways—by Pool Bank, Cowmire Hall, Hodge Hill and Cartmel Fell

CARTMEL COAST

John Wilkinson of Castlehead

From Lindal, Grange, Allithwaite and Flookburgh to Cark and Cartmel

NETHER LEVENS HALL

APPROACH FROM LEVENS BRIDGE

IN the old days travellers averse to the oversands journey from Hest Bank to Kents Bank went north from Lancaster through Carnforth, Milnthorpe, to Levens Hall, where they gazed with interest at "the ancient seat of the Late Duke of Suffolk, where a curious specimen of the old style of gardening may be seen as laid out by the gardener of King James II". They crossed the River Kent at Levens Bridge, thereafter turning west over a wide region of marshy land which covered the upper estuary of the river. Here was a Long Causeway, "laid down over the mosses from Beathwaite Green to the village of Witherslack". The road now is arrow straight; traffic speeds along it and how many road-users even guess that they have missed Nether Levens Hall—the subject of my sketch—surely among the finest of the Westmorland houses, with a ruinous and creeper-clad pele, part of a fourteenth-century barmkyn wall and among the largest cylindrical chimneys to be seen. Its history spans the centuries from the days when Ketel, one of the old Norse landowners, was at Levens in the twelfth century. Its architecture includes building and additions of the fourteenth, sixteenth and seventeenth centuries. As I sat in the sunny farmyard one August afternoon I could not believe in dobbies—local boggarts—nor in tales of a chain-rattling ghost, which were told to me. It is the loveliest plot of seclusion and the Kent flows near by with the gentlest voice.

The highroad takes travellers over the reclaimed marshes to Gilpin Bridge over the Lyth, across a windswept region strangely lovely at times, cried over by flocks of seabirds. Once I saw a score of grey herons winging heavily over Sampool. Always the proud limestone mass of Whitbarrow, a noble monster, dominates the landscape.

West directed the notice of his travellers to Witherslack Black Bull Inn and to the carriage road along the Winster Valley to Newton in Cartmel. He was hotfoot for the Lakes, therefore ignored the charms of the immediate landscape. Witherslack, "the wooded valley" of Norse settlers, is a scattered community with delightful surprises, all nooks and crannies and groups of pretty houses waiting unexpectedly around corners. Town End, with its farms and cottages among hillside damson orchards, is not far from the highroad. More cottages embowered in blossom and flowers are at the roadside going to Church Land and the old church. Ancient farms lie on steeps below church, scars and the Winster river, like one I know with such a ponderous, primitive barn door that the farmer agreed with us on its antiquity, saying, "Yon's a bit of wood old Noah had left over from building the Ark." Some outlying houses have picturesque names — Kirket Nook, Birks, Swimmers, Halecat Cottage, Bellart How, Beck Head. All have some old stone or local wood-carving of age and beauty.

WITHERSLACK CHURCH

The church we approach from Church Lands, where ancient yews and one new "memorial" young tree shade a grass plot, and a seventeenth-century village school and master's house share the sunny silence. Church and school share gratitude to the "Reverend John Barwick, S.D.T. Born in this Hamlet. Late Dean of St. Paul's", who endowed and built them in A.D. 1664. He also left money as dowries for poor maids; and for a new burial ground so that Witherslack dead could be buried in their native earth without the difficult journey to Beetham Church. A story says that once, on his return from the south, Barwick was so distressed to see the neglected state of the old church—which had been allowed to go into decay by local Roman Catholic landlords, the Leyburnes—that he at once vowed to give Witherslack a new chapel.

Barwick's story is interesting, like that of all local boys who make good. Born in 1612 he was educated at Sedbergh School, passed to St. John's College, of which he became a Fellow in 1636.

During the Civil War Barwick was so staunch a Royalist he gave his College plate to the King, for which he was turned out by Cromwell, only to continue spying operations on the Royalist behalf from London. He was imprisoned for his actions and under a cloud during the Commonwealth, but had recovered his fortunes at the Restoration and was able to bequeath so much to his native place.

Witherslack in the sixteenth century belonged to the Broughton family. It was a tradition that at Witherslack was hidden Sir Thomas, who fought for the rebel Lambert Simnel, and as a traitor his life was forfeit. It was said he was buried in or near the old church, but later Broughtons could find no trace of his grave and historians have no opinion to give. Witherslack woods could provide ample hiding-place for wanted men. I know fewer places where it is easier to lose oneself. Thick woods clothe the lower slopes of Whitbarrow Scar. Roads and a mizmaze of bridlepaths wander through them. Sometimes I have felt a wanderer in the true greenwood and half expected to see bowmen clad in green lurking among the aged trees. Old oaks throw shade upon the woodland floor; beeches—as lovely in the silver nakedness of winter as in the green loveliness of May or the red-gold glory of October—split the sunlight into rays. Poplars tremble above secret pools, throwing down their lemon-yellow robes after the first boisterous winds of autumn. Red squirrels sport within the woods, and pheasant are there, jays scream at us like angry fishwives, stockdoves croon and at times a deer passes silently through a glade and is gone so swiftly we wonder—was it imagination? Deer do lurk hereabouts, "small roe deer, no

DOOR AT POOL BANK

bigger nor a dog," says a farmer, "and best inside an oven door. A few steaks off one of 'em and you'd be up Whitbarrow crags before you knew."

Below the woods are the pastures and the level valley of the Winster, a little river which became eastern boundary of the land of Cartmel Priory, and later divided Lancaster North of the Sands from Westmorland, a division remaining to this day. The river, beginning in the fells east of Windermere, flows south—as we saw it at Winster village, to Bowland Bridge, Cowmire Hall, Helton Tarn, under Blea Cragg Bridge and so to Meathop marshes and the Bay.

On the Westmorland side of the river we pass out of the woods to the land around Pool Bank, fields with old names—Carr, Big Moss, Moss End, Bell Meadows, Grigg and Meadow Close, Barley Field, Elsie Meadow, Ireland and Adam's Garden—and peace over all of them. The farm is pushed out into the road, farmyard fowl are "all over t'shop". They prefer the road to the enclosed yard—where I drew the fine wooden gallery over the kitchen door. I drew much more, too, for Miss Brockbank showed me all the house—the vast kitchen, "three steps up", with a plaster overmantel dated I.C.H. 1698, the porch door—its date 1693, fine oak partitions of the muntin and plank type so often used for interior walls where native oak was plentiful, the old doors with their simple wooden latches, the parlour with a fine open fireplace and a ratchet hook to hold a kettle. There is a story that long ago a wife was walled within a living prison in the house—but there is nothing at Pool Bank now to give credence to the gruesome tale. It is full of sunshine and the busy household goes about its work singing. Looking inward all is pleasant. The Hartleys of old times must have been pleasant people; they were the first family to live here.

But the views are the thing; from every window the Winster valley smiles up, or the limestone scars throw back the sun, or there are the deeply shadowed Witherslack Woods. Pool Bank must always have been a most happy dwelling. Every stranger in passing must pause to admire—the sun on the old walls, the yellow hollyhocks against the light grey roughcast—the ancient peace.

A mile away, this time on the Lancashire bank, is Cowmire Hall, a mediæval pele with walls more than four feet thick built to withstand attack from land or sea—raiders were known to

OLD GALLERY—POOL BANK

penetrate inland—fronted by buildings added early in the seventeenth century. What an impressive sight it is, standing four-square in the valley bottom, grey and bare against the wooded slopes of Cartmel Fell. At one time it looked rather sad and neglected, but in 1950 the owner restored it with admirable care; it is no easy task to modernize so ancient a fabric. The pele, for instance, is very much as it always was—double-arched vaults below, where the first builders stored their valuables when danger was imminent and their casks and barrels when troubles were over, and the room above, where the first family lived—their quarters rather cramped, until a hall was built adjoining.

Imagine the difficulties plumbers and electricians had to overcome to adapt it to modern needs—what drilling and boring to introduce pipes through four feet six inches of solid stone wall. Very conveniently the garderobe (in the north-west, and least sunny corner of all castles and peles, the usual form of sanitation) fills one angle of the modern bathroom. When Lt.-Colonel Wellwood showed me his home his three children were playing in their fairy-tale tower, the sun pouring in and fresh sea breezes blowing in at the windows. The Elizabethan addition to the pele has not the solidity of the battlemented tower, it has airs and graces, a splendid oaken staircase with round wooden knobs leading to the upper floor, and a beautiful fireplace in the hall with a design of vine-leaves and grapes all around it; in the design is incorporated the arms of the Flemings, a family with great power in the Rydal-Coniston area long ago. Here, as at Pool Bank, the glazing had been taken out of the parlour windows to avoid the window tax, but again they have been opened out, giving up a little "treasure"—Queen Anne pennies lost by workmen who blocked them.

The Flemings built Cowmire Hall for refuge and security in wild and lawless days; the Hartleys, farmers of the statesmen class, built Pool Bank to keep out only one enemy, the weather, and as in all farms of the period the building was purely functional. The Philipsons who built their house on Hodge Hill, being true Elizabethans, combined good building with art and beauty; their hall is one of the happy surprises of the Winster valley. It looks north and down from its higher position, upon Cowmire Hall, and eastwards across the dale to Pool Bank. As a guest house I think it must be one of the most charming in Lancashire North of the Sands—Hodge Hill Hotel.

PELE—COWMIRE HALL

In 1560 the Philipsons, a family with many estates in

the Windermere country, with their ancient hall at Calgarth, a strong tower for refuge on Belle Isle, and smaller farms at Crook, Causeway, and Ashes east of the lake, built a manor house at Hodge Hill, just below the chapel of Cartmel Fell. An old road toiling over from Kendal and Crosthwaite passed by, and over the heights to the lake-foot fords and Newby Bridge; another ancient road came to its gates from Witherslack. Cowmire Hall was there, frowning over the mosses when the Philipsons came to the manor house, but the new hall was quite unlike the old. No attempt at fortification here, only the new architecture called Elizabethan which produced some of the pleasantest homes for the prosperous squires of the north. Adjoining were farm buildings—the fine barn with its wooden threshing-floor and inner and outer oak-pegged doors is still there—and cart-sheds and stables just as we see at farms like Pool Bank, but here are signs of a family living a different life, with more luxuries at their command—silks and brocade to Pool Bank's honest homespun. In Pool Bank's great kitchen pewter flagons foamed with home-brewed ale—in Hodge Hill's banqueting hall wine-glasses were raised and the toast was "The King—and who'll do him right now". The Philipsons were Royalists—they fought for Charles, like Robin the Devil whose hat is one of the curiosities in Kendal church—and lost much in the cause. The Tudor Philipsons surrounded themselves with dignity and beauty, the lute and virginals were heard in the gracious rooms, their ladies walked in herb gardens and were perfect in the arts of the still-room; they watched their men ride off to war, and turned to the ordering of the household in their absence. Whatever confusion and disorder reigned in the outer world, over the high fells and beyond the sands of the Bay, here within their enclosed gardens all was ordered tranquillity.

So I felt about Hodge Hill as I first saw it. It was such a delightful surprise—all the drowsy sounds of a summer high noon about it, strong blue shadows thrown over the farmyard and brilliant light on roof and chimneys. I noticed the wooden gallery—a not uncommon feature in sixteenth-century Lakeland houses—where maybe "Lucy at her spinning-wheel, in russet gown and apron blue", sat on warm evenings, or where yarn was hung in the days of home industry. Later I stood on the gallery looking at a view which must have been pleasing to the Philipsons, for the landscape included much land which was owned by family and kinsmen, stretching along the Winster to the fells enclosing Windermere, to the Troutbeck valley and Kirkstone Pass.

What has Hodge Hill now to remind us of the early days? Diamonds of blown glass in some of the windows, giving distorted pictures of garden and courtyard, heavy oak beams in the banqueting hall, a beautifully carved seventeenth-century document cupboard and spice cupboards inset within the thick walls; one recess may have been used by some squire of Jacobean times for storing his pipes and precious tobacco, handy by the fireside, panelled walls, oaken partition walls, and at the stair-foot a double dog-gate to prevent the privileged canines of the household stray-

HODGE HILL

ing to the upper rooms. Georgian Philipsons kept small pages to fetch and carry; waiting for orders, the lads sat on the page-boy's seat within a little cupboard at the staircase head. When courting couples sought privacy—when the damp airs from the marshy valley swept over the sequestered garden closes and they were driven indoors, or when, during twelfth-night revelries, two young things stole away from the rest—there was waiting for them, in a dim corner of a long passage, a "spooning seat", a hinged two-seater. When footsteps were heard the same pair could steal out on the spinning gallery and gaze up to the starry skies. The upper rooms possess elegances in keeping with the hall below; there is a fine carved chamber door, B.P.A. 1692; a fair chamber with a powder closet, another with a raised platform which might have served for a page to sleep upon, or keep watch if necessary. All the rooms are delightful, restored so carefully. Old people in the locality remember the same rooms being used to store hay and corn; the fine timber-work and rafters have had coats of paint removed painstakingly from them—the banqueting hall panels had a coat of pink! A stone-paved "hallan" passage runs through the house from front to back, a cool dim place with the sunlit garden seen framed in the porch door. Beyond, bloom roses and a wealth of summer flowers; in February when snow has hardly gone from the far-seen mountain-tops snowdrops are in white drifts on the banks, and two months later the daffodils bloom as only Lakeland daffodils know how. The landscape has a perennial beauty, for it has within it the little dale—in summer fields of waving corn and pastures of well-fed kine stretch across to the woods of Witherslack and they in turn merge with Whitbarrow's crags.

Leaving Hodge Hill to wander downdale by low-level route we soon see still another interesting homestead with a long history, Thorphinsty Hall, named from some old Norseman who settled there nearly a thousand years ago; his wonted path became known as Thorphin's Sty. In Tudor days the Cartwrights began to farm here, and a century later the same Huttons whose graves are thick in the old churchyard on the fell. One, Richard Hutton, remembered the poor of Cartmel Fell in his will, leaving £40 for their aid; the money bought Low House Field—Low House is near Foxfield on the fell above Thorphinsty, and so is Poor House Allotment marked on to-day's maps—the latter possibly being the "three rocky acres of allotment" in church accounts of 1796. Thorphinsty stands high on a hill slope scattered with grey boulders, ranges of large, white-walled buildings and the house itself showing signs of frequent alterations, mullioned windows next to sash windows, chimneys of every local variety, and one door dated 1708 and another 1705. Rambler roses and the pale pinky-yellow tea roses beloved by countryfolk grow on its walls, and yellow poppies flutter around a flagged garden. A delicious "sty"—the word is a "steep path", climbs through hazel and oak copses to a high-level road; nowhere are better blackberries in August. We see them and forget all the roadside flowers which had earlier beguiled the way—willow-herb, campions in deep cerise masses, mountain pansies with petals of deep purple velvet, and scarlet pimpernel, which here, as everywhere, is the poor man's weather glass.

I must say no more of the old homesteads in this valley. Let the others be the happy discoveries of wanderers who, spotting fascinating names on the map, go in search and find unexpected treasures. This is not considered rich country, nor the architectural traditions particularly interesting, but the local craftsmen who built by rule of thumb and as well as they knew how, achieved something which to-day is very, very satisfying. Hardly a farm in the length of the Winster valley but has some feature—usually indoors—recalling the past centuries—court cupboard, aumbry, panelled partition, carved door, oaken staircase.

The Hodge Hill-Thorphinsty road follows the edge of the Winster mosses due south to Lindale and the coastal road we were following from Levens to Grange. The mosses are all drained except for a small tarn called Helton Pool, which we heard about from more than one local farmer before we had been long in the valley. On this pool "first iron ship were tried out", we were told. They mentioned John Wilkinson, whose iron monument is such a feature unmistakable on the highroad near Castlehead.

The story is this. In 1748 John Wilkinson, whose father had been an overlooker in Machell's iron forge at Backbarrow, built or bought his own little forge and furnace down the Winster river at Wilson House, near Lindale. From the Winster mosses he dug peat to use in smelting haematite ore; for ease in transport he cut a canal into the turbary from which he got his peat moss and used a shallow turf-carrying boat. Tradition says Wilkinson made an iron boat, the first of its kind, for this work. One was seen to sink in Helton Pool. Later he adapted his early ideas into making larger vessels of iron; in July 1787 an iron boat was launched and the unbelievers who had scoffed at his claims—forty years earlier Winster folk had also jeered at him: "How dosta think iron'll float?"—were convinced.

Wilkinson was one of Lancashire's inventive geniuses. He had a rich and varied career. Tradition plays a big part in what is told of him. There is a story that he was born in a cart which was carrying his mother to market to sell farm produce, and a prophecy that such a strange beginning was an augury that "John'll be a gurt man". His father made flat-irons as part of his livelihood at Backbarrow. Later John, at Wilson House, invented the box type smoothing-iron, using water power from Lindale Beck to turn the grindstones for the smoothing of the bottoms. He experimented with different methods of smelting haematite ore. He found charcoal from the Winster copses better than peat moss, but having his own turf fields he made good use of the clay deposits beneath them for manufacturing bricks—an innovation in the district. Later he moved to Wolverhampton, and Bilston, still improving the iron trade, inventing a blast furnace, working with the Darbys of Coalbrookdale, carrying out a new water system for Paris which included the laying of 40 miles of pipes—iron ones—inventing an "Iron Man" for boring in coal mines, which might have been adopted but for the fierce opposition of the miners themselves. He built a cast-iron Wesleyan chapel at Bilston, and in his will directed that his body should be carried north to Castlehead in a cast-iron coffin to be interred in the gardens he had created there by the sea. An iron mausoleum was to be erected over his remains. All was done as he wished, but in crossing Morecambe Bay the heavy coffin was almost lost in quicksands and only extricated with difficulty. The cortège finally reached Castlehead. The troubles which were attendant upon Wilkinson's burial are often referred to by local folk. The first iron coffin proving too small to contain inner shells of lead and wood, had to be replaced by a larger—during which time the body was temporarily buried. The grave dug for the second iron coffin was too shallow, so to allow deeper excavation it was disinterred. The twenty-ton-weight iron pyramid was finally placed over the grave and there all thought John Wilkinson would be allowed for all time to rest in peace. But within twenty years the estate changed hands. The mausoleum is no object of beauty and we can understand how the new owners felt about this garden ornament. One night the body of the iron master was again disinterred and a heavy cart carrying the iron coffin moved up the hill to Lindale churchyard.

We shall find out more about Wilkinson when we return to the main road to Grange. The by-way we are travelling at present is Tarn Green Lane, with the pool and its squawking water-fowl below us and the old channel for the turf boats, "The Cut", parallel to our road, proceeding to the valley end at Wilson House Bridge.

One of the loveliest parts of the valley is just ahead, where four lanes end. Leaping down from the fell tops is the fearsome Tow Top or Tautop road—gradient 1 in $3\frac{3}{4}$—from which roadmen warned us off when we first brought the car to the brow head. "It's only fit for them dare-devil motor-cyclists," they told us, and looking down the road with its hairpin bends and rough, stony channels, we agreed whole-heartedly. But to walk down—

that is a different matter, faced with superb views down to the Kent estuary—blue, pale gold and dazzling silver—and to the knotts above Arnside and Warton, and on again to the blue Pennines. Zigzagging down between brackenny banks, wherein hidden sykes and stripling becks chuckle and laugh as they leap between boulders and under rowan tree and holly bush roots, we see the Winster valley growing at the brow foot, a map in greens and browns spread out for us. Autumn is the most colourful season here; at the road edge bracken fronds glitter as if dusted with copper-gold, every slope is afire, the wild cherry, the gean, has leaves of flame, the hollies bear loads of red berries, bushes are festooned with the orange beads of the gadding convolvulus—all is ready for the last flare of splendour before winter comes raging up-channel on the back of the storm-winds. This is an ancient route; travellers who journeyed on foot or on horseback from the Lancaster road towards Ulverston, intent on avoiding the oversands crossing, and others who crossed from Kendal to Winster, were faced with this climbing road. Some must have wished they had risked the perils of the Sands when they saw the arduous journey by land round the bay. When Fletcher Rigge of Cark Hall married his young bride in 1782 and brought her home to the Vale of Cartmel she was so scared by the time they reached the Tow Top road that she refused to live in this dreadful country. She prevailed on her husband to forsake Cartmel and return to live in Northallerton.

Soon after Fletcher Rigge's day the highway surveyors undertook large-scale road works in Cartmel and district. It was a period of enclosures; common lands in the valleys were sold and the moneys spent on improvements, including the surfacing, repairing of public carriage roads—one being from Tow Top road bottom downdale to Lindale, "Back o' th' Fell" road, and another the High Newton, Tow Top, and Holme Common road which crosses the Winster into Westmorland and Witherslack at Blea Crag Bridge. There was a bridge here in Tudor days. In Cartmel Register is a record of a foul murder, and a hanging of the murderer here. In April 1576 "Richard Taylor was buryed, whoe suffered the same day at Blakeragge bridge end for murthering wilfully Rich. Kilner of Witherslack", the site of the hanging being a nearby knoll known as Gallows Hill. To-day the bridge is a sturdy stone structure arching the smooth-flowing river, clear water sliding over green water-weeds and bordered by beeches wherein thrushes and blackbirds sing. An inscription points out that it is the Lancashire-Westmorland boundary, that it is also the border of the parishes of Cartmel and Beetham, that it was rebuilt in 1816.

ON CARTMEL FELL

Before leaving the Winster valley we ought to climb to the fell road, the high-level route, between Tow Top brow head and Cartmel Fell, for it is exhilarating travelling, a scenic route, run-

FRIENDS' MEETING HOUSE—HEIGHTS

ning through typical fell country, bracken, brambles and drystone, boulder-built walls on either hand, or dark pine woods or twinkling copses into which red squirrels disappear, and white-tailed rabbits. On the top stands a grey-walled house half-hidden behind high stone walls—the Heights Friends' Meeting House, with a porch tablet dated 1677, this being the year when George Fox, travelling through Cartmel and the country around Morecambe Bay, found meetings firmly established and organized there. In Sarah Fell's account book I have come across items dealing with the expenses of various members of the Fell family when visiting them: "5/2 spent when Mother went to Lancaster to women's meeting and came home by Cartmel to women's meeting there".

Over the porch is a small room and a look-out window where someone always kept watch during meetings in the days of uncertainty and persecution. In 1699 many Quakers were listed in the parish of Cartmel Fell and over fifty down in the Vale of Cartmel. In 1677 "George Rigg, Edward Stones, Informers, gave intelligence to Miles Dodding (of Conishead Priory, a J.P.) of a meeting which led to 35 being taken and 10 having their goods distrained to the value of £35.17.10., the meeting being held at Height". Distraining: the bailiff came to the homes of the Friends and took away goods to the value of the fine—a heifer, a churn, brass pots, brass pans, pecks of malt or havers (oats) or bigg (barley)—according to the worldly wealth of the householder. To-day, the Meeting House preserves the old peace though the numbers of local Friends have dwindled. Across the road high winds sweep through the trees and comb the grasses of the Friends' burial ground, around the neat rows of headstones—low stones recording but the name, the month and year of death of Teasdales, Hunters, Nashes and Windsors. There were only three burials in about twenty-five years. The owner of the adjoining cottage opened the gate of Heights so that I could make my sketch in the weed-grown garden. He also showed me the Meeting House, the studded porch door, the door-keeper's seat inside, the watcher's room above. Dead leaves ran over a flagged passage divided from the Meeting Room by a roof-high panelled oak partition; an older oaken partition wall divided it from the cottage next door. In 1677 Lawrence Newton gave his barn to Friends for meetings; a carving of 1677 or 1697 is on oak panelling near the raised dais where the elders used to face their fellow Quakers, who sat erect on very narrow, very high benches with high straight backs. The Friends gave up ownership in the 1920's, but Heights remains unchanged, as they left it.

Heights is well named; from the road here we look down to the chequered valley and to the mountains beyond Windermere. Tucked away among the rough fells ahead is the old chapel of the swineherds who toiled long ago for the priory of Cartmel. Finger-posts point to "The Church", but it does not seem eager to discover its whereabouts; heather-clad hill-tops crowd around, they enclose enchanted hollows carpeted with smoothest turf, and grey rocks and tumbled boulders create exquisite rock-gardens where Nature and none other is the gardener. Delicious scents—pine scent, larch, heather flower, sweet fern, bog myrtle—rise on the breeze; sheep trods wind in and out of the hollows, and green paths with some purpose we follow, hoping to track down the elusive St. Anthony's. We hear the sound of shrill voices which gives us our bearings; near the church is the little school—and it is playtime. Small children have trodden out the more purposeful paths in and out of the hollows, generations of them, and the feet of parishioners bound to the church. For centuries this fell top has been a focal centre. The great folk of Cowmire and Hodge Hill came here, the families from Thorphinsty Hall and a score of scattered fell farms, on horseback, their womenfolk pillion behind them. They alighted within the churchyard, beyond the great yews, and threw the reins over a tethering-post near the south door. Their dogs followed them in, close at heel, and crouched under the benches upon the rush-strewn floor. The

ST. ANTHONY'S—CARTMEL FELL

wealthy landowners sat within their fine screened pews, the lesser folk occupied narrow benches in the body of the church.

The "cage" pews of the great, the fine three-decker pulpit, the ancient glass in the east window are treasures of this otherwise simple and unadorned house of God. From time to time relics of olden times come to hand. Once a man was discovered poking the fire with a very unusual instrument. On examination it was found to be a carved wooden figure of Christ crucified; it is now in the vestry.

A hospice for the good of the swineherds and herders of Cartmel Fell probably existed here from the early days of the priory and it is likely some holy man, whose isolated cell made him appear as a hermit in the eyes of outsiders, served the spiritual needs of the people. The present building was not the first on the lonely site. It was built at the beginning of the sixteenth century, not many years before the Reformation. The congregation must always have been simple, untutored folk and I think it more likely that a strange tale told by John Shaw of Yorkshire and quoted in *Curiosities of Literature,* by Disraeli's father, belongs to Cartmel Fell Church rather than to Cartmel Priory. Shaw, a Puritanical divine, preached at Cartmel which was then —so he claimed—"without minister". Among his auditors was a man of Cartmel aged sixty who did not know how many gods there were, wanted to know how he could be saved, and had only heard the name of Christ in Kendal "in a play called 'Corpus Christ's Play', where there was a man on a tree and blood ran down". Such ignorance was improbable in a dweller near the Priory, which as parish church in the years after the dissolution was never without its chaplains. The man, of course, might have been a half-wit.

It is 3.30, almost home time at the school. A small girl appears at the door to recall a scattering of small boys with, "It's 'ymn time. You've got to come in." A silence falls within the building, then a tinkling tune on a piano, and "Now the day is over" sung by voices high and low, clear and sweet, gruff and grunting. A minute later there is a rush of feet and the children scatter. Now the day is over? Not it—it is only just beginning! They scramble up and over the rocks, slide down on their behinds—sensible mothers have reinforced trouser seats with leather patches —and halloo and shout as they disappear into the rock-walled hollows. Later we see them dispersing along the roads and tracks to lonely farms out of sight of highroad and valley. One night each month their mothers trudge along the same tracks to the Women's Institute, held in the school; once the W.I. used a room at Hodge Hill.

We have a choice of still higher routes when we wander above the Winster—exciting tracks coiling over Ravensbarrow into the old coach road on Gummers How, another wonderful fell walk by Rankthorn to Foxfield and over Chapel House plantation and Cop o' Cow Hill to Staveley and Windermere foot and Lakeside landing. What delightful solitudes this track penetrates—through elfin copses, over babbling becks, across upland hollows where bog myrtle scents the air, along miles of soft turf-carpeted paths "O'er t'lots". For the true lover of lonely places here is felicity indeed. The heights reached, the lake appears—Winander-mere with all its "neuks and nabs".

CARTMEL COAST—LINDALE, GRANGE TO FLOOKBURGH

We now return to the main Grange highroad at the Witherslack road end, where we left it. Not far from the Derby Arms the road ceases to hug the scar edge and strikes across the mouth of the valley to Wilson House, scene of John Wilkinson's early labours, and over the river at Wilson House Bridge. All this was

MILL POND—LINDALE

once marsh, often inundated by high tides which made islands of the low mounds at Meathop and Ulpha and of Castlehead rock. Two centuries ago all was wilderness and wasteland, until Wilkinson came along, bought the promontory and with his wonted energy and zeal made the desert blossom as the rose. Castlehead was barren rock; he had loads of soil transported in panniers slung over horses so that gardeners could create beauty. It was not labour unknown to him. When he was a lad at Backbarrow he helped his father to level outcrops of rock behind his home whereon they could grow fruit, espalier peach, plum and pear trees. When workmen were digging foundations for his mansion they unearthed relics of prehistory which proved fascinating study for John Wilkinson's learned and scientific friends. They found coins, British and Roman, trinkets worn by native women, beads, rings, amulets, fragments of glass which must have come from some Roman building. After Wilkinson's death the antiquities were sold to a Liverpool Jew, and disappeared.

Just beyond the lodge of Castlehead, Wilkinson's cast-iron monument, rejected by the Mucklows, who came to live here, has found a new home. An inscription reads thus: "John Wilkinson, Ironmaster, died July 14th, 1808, aged 80. His different works in various parts of the kingdom are lasting testimonies of his unceasing labours. His life was spent in action for the benefit of Man and, as he presumed, humbly, to hope, to the Glory of God. *Labore et Honore.*" This does not sound like the epitaph of an atheist, though local folks who talk about him dwell upon his atheism, and upon the sensational details of the several burials of the famous iron coffin.

Lindale has been sadly torn apart by road widenings where two highways meet. The old highway went uphill and down through the village. These old through routes used to be quiet by-ways under the garden walls of pretty houses with roses and honeysuckle round their porches, and masses of pink and blue hydrangeas at their doors. There is the old Mill House reflected in the still waters of the pond, and Milldam Cottage with an old lady smiling down from her front door. By the Corn Mill noisy tumbling becks and mill stream provide Lindale with constant water music—cheerful accompaniment to all the bird-song of a summer evening. The Institute is at the bottom of a hilly street, the school at the top and, on again, the church. This is not the same building in which George Fox "spoake" during his first journey through north Lancashire in 1652—the church was enlarged in 1760 and largely rebuilt in 1829—but he came along the same wandering roads which we may walk between Staveley and Newton-in-Cartmel. His journal tells how he came in the afternoon of his visit to "Priest Camelford's chapell" at Staveley, to Lindale, where in "the steeple house or chapell when ye priest had done" he spoke to a congregation at first hostile, but which "after came to be convinct".

From the churchyard we look to the village huddled down below, over fruitful orchards—what a country for fruit, especially damsons, that is—over grey roofs to the shining millpond; from the nearby War Memorial hill the landscape is one of the most charming in Cartmel, a symposium of village England. Behind us the road climbs Lindale Brow to the new highroad to Newby

Bridge, one of the busiest north of the Sands. We can hear the hum of heavy traffic crawling up the hill to Nether Newton. A little from the roadside we can see farmhouses, Eller How, Moss End and Buck Crag, all with their backs to rocky fell slopes.

Buck Crag bred a family of more than ordinary character. The sons of this quite small farm became the great clerics in the eighteenth century. Edmund Law was curate at the little church of Staveley-in-Cartmel, teaching the village children also, as was usual in the eighteenth century, his salary being but "twice £10

FARM AT BUCK CRAG

a year", doubtless helped out by Whittlegate and gifts in kind from parishioners and the parents of his scholars. He walked daily from Buck Crag to Staveley—eight miles—and as his curacy lasted from 1693 to 1742 he covered some miles. He had a son, born at the farm in 1703, who became Master of Peterhouse, Cambridge—he, too, travelled far—and later was Lord Bishop of Carlisle with Rose Castle as his palace. His sons distinguished themselves; John Law became Bishop of Elphin, Edward was created Baron Ellenborough—a son of his was a Governor General of India—and George, Bishop of Bath and Wells. A story is told of one of these grandsons of Edmund the curate, who returned to his ancestral home to meditate upon the honest simplicity which had been the background of his family two generations earlier. He sat himself down by the inglenook in his father's chair, making a mental picture to carry away with him—but he did not carry away the chair, although he much wanted it for himself.

Grange-over-Sands a century ago was only a very small community of fishermen whose whitewashed cottages shone out at the foot of Hampsfell, a welcome sight to the travellers who saw them from the Sands. They knew the Guide's House at Cart Lane was not far away. With the coming of the Furness Railway, Grange became more accessible; visitors in search of pleasant retirement, mild climate, found it to their liking. Victorian villas began to spread along the edge of the Bay and uphill towards the fell. They had gardens where flowers grew in superabundance, they surrounded their walls with masses of colour. The town also decided to make a garden of the land alongside the railway—sheltered by the embankment. To-day the ornamental lakes with their water-fowl, the rock-gardens, the tree-shadowed paths, are the pride of Grange and the pleasant loitering-places of summer visitors. If the beauty should pall there is always the promenade on the seaward side of the railway and a scene across the bay austere in its clear outline and purity of colour. When last I was there, an autumn night with a sky full of stars sparkling in the keen air, a full moon was riding over Castle Head, moonlight reflected on wet sand and wet mud; the beauty was magical, beauty estranged, a memory to carry away and remember.

When Edwin Waugh walked through Grange in 1860 it was a place so little visited and its villagers so rustic that "they eyed me", he wrote, "from head to foot, wondering where I came from".

Grange-over-Sands in 1860 was beginning to realize that a new period of prosperity was coming with the Furness Railway. The rustic population of woodcutters and fishermen was to give way as the years passed to an entirely different class of resident. The fisherfolk are still in evidence along Cart Lane, where the cottages straggle along to Kents Bank and Guide's House Farm, the home of a Sands' guide to-day, one who was proud as a servant of the Duchy of Lancaster to meet King George VI in 1951 when he visited the county as its Duke. Duties are now less onerous than those of his forbears, whose guiding of over-sands travellers was a full-time job. Only rambling societies call upon the present guide to see them safely across the dangerous and changeable Kent channels, the end of an exciting journey over Morecambe Bay from Hest Bank. This same crossing had for centuries been a commonplace; many tourists bound for Lakeland used it and continued from the shore at Kents Bank north to Cartmel, as we shall do.

Inland from Kents Bank is the sunny, flower-adorned village of Allithwaite, a charming little place, not far from the tremendous promontory Humphrey Head. Here in fabulous days fairies had their castlet and their fairy wells, here the last wolf was driven to its death at the end of a wonderful chase—after which, according to a ballad, the hero of the exploit won for his bride the fair Adela of the nearby hall, Wraysholm Tower. On the shore the much-visited Holy Well, where Northumberland miners came for the cure and the curious imbibed the potent waters down the the centuries, is now hidden within a locked shed and to drink we have to scoop water from the pools in the sand. The sea winds blow and seabirds cry around us; westwards stretches the great level Winder Moor, with the West and East Plains which were won from the swamps and the waves early in the last century—and won back again in part by the sea. Lanes wander over the plains. On them we meet fisherfolk, mostly cocklers and shrimpers coming down from Flookburgh to follow the tides in their tractors, as their fathers did before them in their carts. They are quiet, even dour folk, and go about their business calmly and deliberately, spreading out over the sands and filing into the channels at the ebb-tide. Perhaps they still believe that a quarrel or a fight upon the sands would lead to the disappearance of the shrimps from the local beds—and so save their disagreements for another time and place.

Flookburgh, where many of the fishermen live, is a place of great antiquity honoured by the grant of a charter as long ago as the days of Edward I—the same great king who came this way over-sands to the border and Scotland, there to give the enemy a hammering. Once the people were lawless, wild, descendants—so they say—of pirates and smugglers. Now they are a different breed of men, but they still pit their strength against the elements and the sea. At harvest festivals they drape the pulpit in the new church with a fishing net and thank God for the harvest of the sea, which means more to them than the crops of the fields and the fruits of the orchards—though they remember these too. Corn waves over Winder Moor in August, and almost every garden in Flookburgh has orchard boughs laden with fruit in September. Flookburgh's neighbour and age-old rival is Cark, where once men built ships for northern seas at the mouth of the Eea and from whence in the early days of the railway "a thousand tons of cockles were sent each year to the south Lancashire towns".

From Grange we can go on to Allithwaite, discover Wraysholm's mediæval tower, wander through old Flookburgh, then north to Cark where a most charming stream enters Leven Sands—the same stream which waters the Vale of Cartmel. And Cark is very near to its better-known neighbour, Cartmel Town.

TO HAMPSFELL HOSPICE

Do you know Hampsfell—that exhilarating height behind and north of Grange-over-Sands which turns a smooth turf-clad shoulder towards Cartmel Priory and thickly wooded steeps towards Lindale? It is definitely a place to climb for the view; folk have been doing so for a century—since early Victorian days when picnics and prospects were a most popular combination. They were still doing it on the very lovely morning I ascended thither; in their scores they climbed. But none tried my way.

I came from the beautifully tree-shadowed highway near a house called Slack. Brilliant sunshine beat fiercely outside the belt of trees. A sign was there clearly saying "Public Footpath to Hampsfell" and showing the way to a most delightful, inviting, climbing path—"a tunnel of green gloom" dappled here and there with sun patches. This promised well—the shade I crave, delicious damp earth scents and peeps into a completely wild wood. I turned right, then was tempted by an alluring path to the left, climbed up and up, realized the path was changing character, narrowing as it climbed, footfalls deadened by the accumulated leaf mould of years. I disentangled my hair from hazels, pulled aside low boughs, wove my way between scrub oaks and secret hollies, scrambled over tree roots and decayed stumps all completely "mossy moot". And all the time I climbed and the woodland climbed too. There were walls of rock and miniature limestone scars.

I realized this was not the public footpath to Hampsfell, but knowing I was somewhere on Hampsfell's eastern slopes I kept up and on. I must, thought I, see sky soon.

But no sky appeared. I bethought me of tales of folk lost in forests. Later I found that these were Eggerslack Woods, "carefully cultivated for bobbin wood, hoops, wickerwork, and a great source of employment for people around". So Waugh wrote in 1860.

Later I saw light. Round a rock face trees thinned. I entered a brackenny place humming with insect life, the sun blazed down, the sky was blue above and looking over a stone wall were a dozen elderly people, all of whom had gently perspired up the public footpath and were—for probably the tenth time—stopping to admire the view. They would stop ten times more before they reached the Hospice. The end was not yet in sight.

The open fell was there, its herbage a close-knit lawn of emerald turf sprinkled with eyebright, bedstraw and tormentil, and purple carpets of wild thyme there to be trodden so that the perfume might mingle with the salt tang of the sea. Wild thyme grew over the limestone slabs grooved and eroded by water into the most fantastic animal shapes. Half the garden walls in this part of Lancashire have extraordinary bestiaries embedded in concrete, most of them riven from the limestone of Grange Fell.

As I climbed, gradually now, over the outcropping limestone, I found the fell swarming with folk and all bound for the Victorian view-tower on the highest point—the Hampsfell Hospice. And what a friendly place it is, as its builder hoped.

The Hospice is a perfect early Victorian period piece, a stone tower 729 feet above sea level, a shelter provided with stone benches below and a roof approached by stone steps from which one surveys the prospect and names natural features by means of a most ingenious viewfinder. There is nothing exceptionally beautiful about the place (apart from site or views) nor of any outstanding historic importance, unless we recall the amusing incident known as "Hampsfield Feyt", when the very timorous, chicken-hearted men of Cartmel assembled on the fell top waiting for a messenger to come galloping over-sands to set their minds at rest about the fear of Jacobite rebels disturbing their peace.

But I was interested to learn two facts—that the Hospice founder was Mr. Remington, who once lived at Longlands Hall and climbed to this place every morning before breakfast, and that the Indicator was a labour of love made by a retired railway man, Mr. Garstang, who loved this fell top as dearly.

Inside the shelter is a very amusing series of painted boards carrying verses obviously devised by the Victorian gentleman who built the Hospice.

The verses and admonitory notices—one a beauty about vandals and litter louts "who possess more muscle than brain"—I dearly craved for my collection of "collectible curiosities". I said this was a friendly place. The boisterous wind which blew us all around did something to break down barriers and bring about the extremely brotherly hopes of the builder.

"And if the rich and poor should meet
I trust they will each other greet."

One very handsome old gentleman lent me a gold pencil and a youth ripped open a used envelope he found in a blazer pocket that I might copy them down. The three of us had the revolving viewfinder to play with—a round table top on a pedestal with numbers round the rim. We collaborated; one squinted along a movable "arm", pointed it at the distant mountain peaks, found their numbers on the rim whilst another found corresponding names for the numbers on a chart. It was great fun. The view was superb. We might have spent an hour identifying scores of mountains and fells—Lakeland and Pennine—but other people were being blown to the roof top by the wind and all were anxious for a turn with the viewfinder.

"The roof will show a prospect rare."

So the verses declare—

"The noble bay and stealthy tides
That treacherous creep along the sand."

All Morecambe Bay is spread out—silver and gold—below us, but not with "gaily rigged trim pleasure boats" as in 1846.

We tore ourselves away, descended slowly, for "a flight of steps requireth care", and with gold pencil and envelope I proceeded to copy the verses within the tower.

Time was passing. I saw a green path south to the fell end. I idled along, inhaling odours sweet, enjoying every moment. I heard the sonorous striking of a church clock from the valley to my right—Cartmel Priory telling the world it was noon. It told me I must leave the fell and descend with all speed. I made a bee-line for Cartmel—zigzagging down the slopes to Aynsome and the valley.

TO CARTMEL AND THE PRIORY

If we have any doubts about the charms of Old Cartmel as we pass out of Cark and on the road to the Priory they will be dispelled as soon as we look upon Cark Hall, the first of many gracious and lovely old halls in the Eea valley. Its masonry is primrose-hued like the Priory stone; its walls bulge over the highway, the foundations built on boulders and bedrock; orchard trees bend their boughs towards the wayfarer, and across the road is the bustling, rushing millstream side by side with the slower-moving, crystal-clear waters of a little river—Cartmel's own stream—we shall see so many times as we travel north to Newby Bridge.

It was a sunny day when I sketched the fine seventeenth-century doorway of Robert Rawlinson's house, with the arms displayed above with obvious pride. The earlier hall of Cark was the home of Pickerings in Tudor times, a daughter marrying Elizabeth's cup bearer, Robert Curwen. Their nephew, a Rawlinson, inherited Cark and in Stuart times the family, and their friends, walked about in the front garden—called a Pleasaunce—and discussed politics with great animation. The Restoration was a matter of family interest, for the wife of Curwen Rawlinson was niece of General Monk, instrumental in the King's return. Curwen became Justice of His Majesty King Charles II, who granted him the arms. He knew well that uncomfortable man, George Fox, when in his legal office he met him at Holker Hall. Not at all intimidated he sent him to Lancaster Castle. His wife's memorial in the Priory tells how she died "from the tortures of ye stone". Their elder son, called Monk, died young and his brother Christopher, a fine antiquarian and scholar, died a bachelor, so Cark Hall passed to cousins, the Rigges. Rigges came to Cark as a fine completed hall and liked it well enough, but a newly married wife of Fletcher Rigge, coming here over the fearsome hill

CARK HALL

of Tow Top, was so terrified by the journey and so appalled at the Eea valley desolation she vowed nothing would make her live there. She won her way. Some years later the foul roads were much improved—in fact the excellent state of the eighteenth-century roads, which are such a network over the Vale of Cartmel, amazes me. When the planners of the roads insisted they should be "20 feet wide between fences" and that roads and bridges were to be chargeable to local ratepayers there was an outcry. It would "send them all to beggary", they said.

Stockdale, the historian of Cartmel, tells an amusing story of

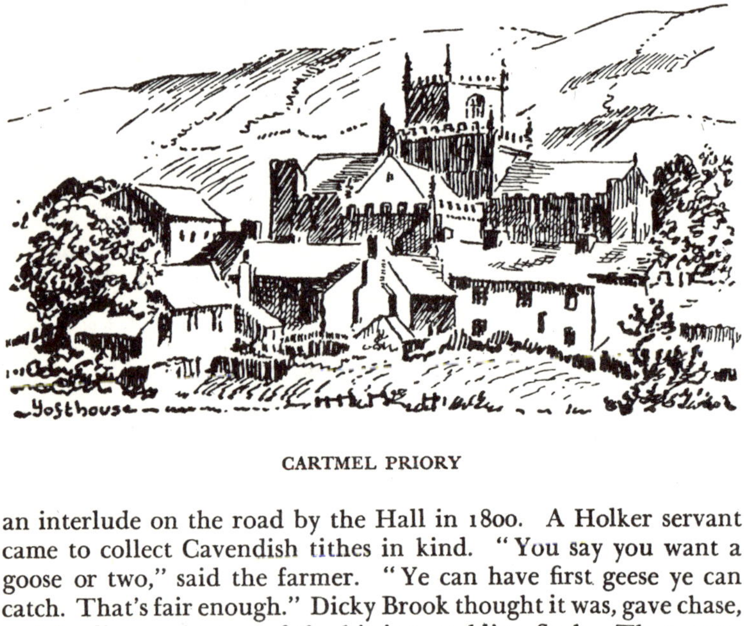

CARTMEL PRIORY

an interlude on the road by the Hall in 1800. A Holker servant came to collect Cavendish tithes in kind. "You say you want a goose or two," said the farmer. "Ye can have first geese ye can catch. That's fair enough." Dicky Brook thought it was, gave chase, and finally caught two of the hissing, cackling flock. They were, naturally, the least active and weakliest birds, as he described them, "Yan wi but yae leg and t'other leet as a seeah maaew"—that is, light as a sea-mew.

The highroad goes north to Cartmel through the gentle green valley to the four roads end at Headless Cross where inset in the wall is a stone of interest to travellers of long ago. "Oversands to Lancaster 15 miles. Oversands to Ulverston 7 miles", it reads.

More exciting approaches to Cartmel are from Holker, a footway from the village by Hole of Ellel Farm, by a wood edge—where sweet chestnuts are there for the picking in November, and up to the top of Holker Bank. The backward views over Winder Moor, the coast and the Bay are lovely. As the tide ebbs you can see shrimpers' carts fanning out over the shining wet sands.

Tracks climb from our direct way to the high, round-topped hill, Mount Barnard, called by some the Holy Hill, for it was thereon, high above the world, the first brethren came to build a house of God. A vision made them seek a new site—and of that I will tell when we reach Cartmel. Paths climb through new plantations to the crown of beeches, a charmed circle of them within which you can stand in cloistered calm, though it is not easy to look out through the screen of trees to the outside world. From every point of the compass and from far away you can see this tree-crowned hill-top, a splendid landmark. One small Cartmel child once thought it was the real "green hill far away".

The track goes through more woods and over lush pastures to the Park where suddenly comes that wonderful view of the tower rising above the clustered roofs of Cartmel. The scene is not always so peaceful as my sketch shows. Come on the day of Cartmel's Whitsun Races or to the Show in August—and what a milling crowd of people! Long ago the Park was a place for local gatherings. Stockdale refers to a stone here where bulls were baited, and tells of wrestling matches where Cartmel men settled bitter quarrels in the most manly way they knew, and of rowdy scenes within the Park ending in affrays and blood-wipes. Gatherings are more peaceable nowadays.

Beyond the stream we pass between the first houses in the village and at once find ourselves at the heart of Cartmel. The soul is just beyond. The Priory church clock strikes above the quietness blending with the striking of hammer on anvil from the smithy. There is the post office-cum-grocer-cum-greengrocer-cum tea and coffee merchant at the corner, the Priory Guest House with its overhanging upper rooms supported on round pillars, a bank, tiny, made to measure, squeezed in between Guest House and Royal Oak, and there is the King's Arms and the gracious eighteenth-century Priory Hotel—from both of which guests can watch the world go by. In between and round the square are shops, pleasant Queen Anne and Georgian houses rich with atmosphere, overlaid with dignity, with neat doors, discreetly curtained windows. And in mid-square is the focal-point where children play, elders sit and gossip and the bus draws up with a flourish.

"Damme," exclaimed an old man who talked to me as I made my sketch of the Priory gateway, "this place gets more like Lunnon every day!" A bus had just drawn up and disgorged a score of visitors.

Old and new have come to terms in this old place. Time has used it kindly. In 1860 Edwin Waugh described life here after the city "like going to bed". He did, however, commend the

PRIORY GATEHOUSE—CARTMEL

catering at the King's Arms. "I asked a man with a red nose where I could get a glass of good ale—I found hungry wood-cutters sitting within waiting for a great dish of lobscouse prepared by the handsome good-natured landlady. . . . They finished off with oatcake, butter and cheese and crisp water-cresses."

The Priory Gateway, the only monastic building remaining —apart from the church and a few lengths of precinct wall—used to keep intruders out of the Priory precincts. Now it is an invitation to explore beyond. But first—into the gatehouse which is National Trust property. Climbing wide, spiralling, stone steps built by fourteenth-century masons, we come to a fine chamber, with windows containing stone tracery—and framing fascinating peeps of the streets below. An artist has his studio within, lining the walls with local and Lakeland landscapes.

This gateway played an important role in pre-Reformation times, and in the seventeenth century the upper room served as the Grammar School. On one occasion it became a tower of refuge, filled to overflowing with scared Cartmoelians, male and female, determined to be the last to fall to the ferocity of the Scots. They were not living in the days of border raids, nor in the period of The Bruce's hit-and-run campaigns, but in 1745 when every northern community was busily organizing some sort of defence against the advance of the Jacobite rebels. Cartmel began boldly enough. All able men assembled with any weapons available—likely and unlikely ones—on the summit of Hampsfell, their womenfolk and all the excited youngsters tagging on behind, eager to miss nothing of the fun. Let them get at the rebels, they boasted. One of them, Harry Barwick, who owned fleet racehorses—the valley from mediæval days was known for horse breeding, and its pastures still carry an unusual number of fine bloodstock—was told off to speed over the sands to find out how far the rebels had marched and to come back with all haste to inform the local "army", who would then "take steps". What steps they would have taken no one will ever know. After long waiting watchers on the fell did spot a galloping horse on the sands approaching Cart Lane, a coatless and hatless horseman upon his back. Someone must have voiced a fear that Barwick was in sore straits. The next man cried Barwick was fleeing for his life. Someone else shouted that the Scots were behind their messenger, that they would be coming in sight any minute. In a trice Hampsfell was cleared. No one waited long enough to make sure if the rebels were indeed crossing the Bay. They tumbled downhill, raced for Cartmel, and once in the safety of their own alleys and homes they barricaded them and waited. The more timorous villagers and the overflow made for the Gatehouse, a sure defence. Barwick, after a while, rode into the square to report, saw not a soul stirring. According to the local story an old woman was the first to show herself—from the Gatehouse topmost window. Were the Scots at Headless Cross yet? More white faces appeared and doors opened an inch or two. Soon Harry Barwick was railing at them for a set of cowards "with no pluck at 'a—only fit to make flay-craaes [scarecrows] of". He had not been all the way to Milnthorpe, as they thought, but had ridden away and then returned "as if the devil was at his heels" intending to scare them, to see "what soort o' mettel they wor maied on". Fortunately the Scots army came no nearer than Burton in Kendal and Carnforth as it went south the next day.

Cartmel is full of old folk and pleasant folk who stop to talk. They are slow, unhurried. Time matters little it would seem. One summer afternoon as I sketched my way around I had company all the while, from a small boy who joined me on the fish stones, decided he would draw too and returned from a nearby house complete with paper and an assortment of coloured pencils, to the man with a scythe mowing the dog daisies in the churchyard, and an elderly exile back to her native Cartmel from a south Lancashire town. There were others too who passed on odd scraps of information relating to Cartmel's past.

The old woman recalled Cartmel of ninety years ago when "it cost twopence a week to go to school and if you forgot your school-pence you were sent home". On Sunday, dressed in frocks kept only for church and Sunday school, they recited the Collect for the Day to their teachers, earning as reward the coveted blue ticket. A little girl in the 1870's was always eager to run errands for old ladies; she was given a slice of bread and jam as payment, but for fetching and carrying water from the Parson's Well by Pepper Bridge for an invalid granny she was given twopence a week. In summer whole families of children were hired out to local farmers. "We all went turnip thinning when I was about seven. We got twopence a row from the farmer—and our mother used to send us to the farm for a quart of blue milk. We were brought up hard."

Almost everyone will tell about the Whitsuntide Races and the August Show—outstanding events in Cartmel's year, but only the old have anything to say about Cartmel Fair, when the great cattle, sheep and horse sales were held in the main street, or the Tuesday markets. Only one link remains with the old days; Tuesday is still the day when the branch bank does its local business.

From another I heard facts connected with a most interesting charity which is still divided out among local poor, money derived from four fields near the Grange Fell road, rented by Mr. Brocklebank for £18. Has any charity a more exciting name than that of Beggar's Breeches? The story is not without interest. In January 1799 Mr. Robinson, coming from the Backbarrow Cotton Works over the fell to Broughton, found a poor person who called himself William Fearns lying helpless in the snow. A cart was sent from Broughton to carry the man to the overseer at Cartmel where he was refreshed with tea and gin, taken to a lodging-house, and a doctor brought in—Mr. Brockbank, the surgeon. The man complained of his poverty, but refused to allow the overseer to send news to a son he claimed to have at Condor Green near Lancaster, even though his life was in danger. He died, as all thought, penniless. No son was found to live at Conder Green, and no relatives traced. In the Lancashire Record Office is the Upper Holker Township Book with the overseer's account in full. "At his passing away Richard Chapman's wife sent for me as her husband was from home, and after he died, on taking off his breeches—which he would never suffer to be taken off while alive—they felt very heavy; on examining them a bag was found in the Fob which contained One Hundred and Eighty-Five Guineas and a Half in gold which astonished us all present, all which it was supposed he had got by begging; he travelled the country with a certificate which he had somehow procured from St. Thomas' Hospital, London, and pretended he had been cut for the stone and showed a small stone which he said was extracted from his Bladder . . . We found he was an impostor." No one appeared with sufficient claim to be given the beggar's money, therefore land was bought and the poor of the Township of Upper Holker in Cartmel still benefit.

In Cartmel are names from monastic times, South Cross, more often called Headless Cross to-day, where weary pilgrims thanked God for safe passage of the Sands and lifted up their hearts as they saw their goal—the Priory, in sight; Priory Close, a gracious House, traditionally the house of the Prior of Cartmel; Tithe Barn and Barngarth, the Friarage and the Farmery date from pre-Reformation days, but Parson's Well from later times. Here we find a stone well in an angle of the wall by a clear stream; carriers of water used to cross a stone slab to reach it and as they filled their pails gossiped with watchers on Pepper Bridge.

The stone bridge and the well in the wall are still there, and the stream flows north, passing the east end of the Priory graveyard. Go along the north churchyard wall and beyond the Priory is yet another bridge and another stream, this one flowing southwards. The monks built their great monastic house between the two—and on the north and south flow of these inconsiderable streams hinges the legend of the founding of the Priory.

All around Cartmel are clear streams—the River Eea, Middlefield Beck and Clogger Beck; the streets and lanes have many little bridges—there is Pepper Bridge, Wheelhouse Bridge, Church Bridge and others too insignificant to be named.

In A.D. 1188 the great William Mareshal, Earl of Pembroke, gave all the Cartmel lands he had received from Henry II to the canons of St. Augustine to found a Priory, "giving and granting it every kind of liberty that heart can conceive or mouth utter. Whosoever shall infringe or injure, may he incurr the curse of God, the Blessed Virgin Mary and all other saints, as well as my malediction." So far, so good—but where was the Priory to be built? A story says that "120 foreign monks" arrived on the scene and decided to build on the hill-top known as Mount Barnard or St. Bernard's Mount—a lovely green hill it must have looked to them—but a voice, a vision of St. Cuthbert, sent them downhill. "Not here, but in a valley between two rivers, where one goes north and the other south", they were commanded to build. The present site fitted the bill and there the Priory took shape.

THE PRIORY

Is there any picture more beautiful than a familiar landscape transfigured into something rare and strange by the first fall of snow?

I have in my mind's eye a picture of the Vale of Cartmel after a snowfall, the drifts of autumn leaves by laneside at Field Broughton and Longlands now lost under drifts of snow. At the valley head the mountains are all snowy giants; at the valley mouth rises the great tower of the Priory, its turrets and battlements white-edged, proud against a clear blue sky. It is Sunday morning and the sound of church bells is blown in sweet bouts towards us—the same bells of which Gordon Bottomley wrote in his poem "New Year's Eve", "ringing out an aged past":

> "O Cartmel bells, ring soft to-night,
> And Cartmel bells ring clear——"

Cartmel on a Sunday morning in winter is very different from the busy village we know so well in summer, when troops of Boy Scouts and Girl Guides march in order to morning service, and fleets of buses from Grange bring in scores of visitors to augment the native congregation. On August Sabbaths the spacious nave is thronged with worshippers, and transepts too—but in winter only the faithful from village and scattered houses by the River Eea trudge through the snow. Before the bells have ceased ringing the last old ladies have stamped off the snow from their shoes in the porch, the last children have raced through the Square and taken their places beneath the soaring pillars. When they sing, the voices are faint and thin, the sound rises to the high roof to mingle with the echoes caught there over long centuries. Shafts of cold sunlight pierce the gloom, and the pale, primrose-tinted stone takes on an unearthly pallor.

What a noble edifice Cartmel Priory is, a gem of architecture which arose complete and splendid at a time when all around was savage, untamed country—marshland below, waste fells above—land where only a few scattered communities of cowherds and shepherds, tenants and servants of the Prior, earned a subsistence. Long ago, when history was just taking shape in Cumbria, a King of Northumberland gave "Cartmel and all the Britons in it" to St. Cuthbert, and amid all the changes brought about by raiding Norsemen, Norman conquest and the coming of Norman barons to claim grants of land in the north-west, Cartmel remained in the possession of the Church. When the extent of Cartmel was defined in the thirteenth century—at the time when Furness Abbey was also a great power in the land—it was given as the wedge between the Winster river and Windermere; to the north, Wrynose and the Brathay river, to the west, the Leven and Cartmel Sands marked the border of Furness.

The Prior had water mills at Newby Bridge and at Backbarrow, fishing rights all along the coast, and provided the guide at Kents Bank to show travellers over the Kent channel, and he in turn paid a second guide for the Keer channel. All the farms from Lindale to Cartmel Fell were theirs, and swineherds had their booths in the same wild hills; in the Vale of Cartmel they carried on horse-breeding, around Hampsfell and High Cark fells; on Newton and Bigland fells were vast sheep-walks.

The Priory belonged to the Black Canons, the Canons Regular of St. Augustine, an order less austere and with greater freedom than that enjoyed by the monks of Cistercian houses such as Furness or Whalley. No "outsiders" entered the monastic churches of the Cistercians, but from the beginning the parishioners of Cartmel worshipped in part of the Priory Church set apart for them, a fact which saved it from destruction after the Dissolution in 1536. This also happened at Bolton Priory—the church being saved in part for the use of the people as a parish church. In orders given for the dissolution of Cartmel is a query—"The Church of Cartmel, being the Priorie, and also P'sh Church, whether to stand unplucked down or not?" The answer came from the Chancellor of the Duchy, "Ordered—to stand still." So the church still stands, but not quite as it was when the Prior and brethren left it. The Prior stayed in the district to farm the rectory; the cellarer became the new vicar. The villagers now had their own church and, something new, the responsibility for its upkeep. But they were very poor.

For seventy years and more the church became more and more decayed—the roof was in a parlous state, the choir neglected, the woodwork rotted, the windows without glazing—some of the mediæval stained glass had found its way to churches at Bowness and Cartmel Fell—and everywhere sore need for repair. The parishioners came to the rescue, but above all, Mr. George Preston, of Holker Hall, whose restoration in its way shows craftsmanship as fine as that of the mediæval workmen. The roof, the wonderful screens and canopies behind the choir stalls, carved with the symbols of the Passion of Our Lord, are his best memorial. Cartmel folk were rightly proud of their church when all was complete. Then came the Civil War, Cromwellian soldiers stabling their horses in the fine, newly roofed nave, smashing glass windows, breaking maliciously the organs "of great value", one of Mr. Preston's gifts—no wonder the angered villagers cried out against the desecration. And tradition says that the bullet-holes still to be seen were made when men of Cartmel shot at the Puritan vandals in 1643.

Days of strife are forgotten. The Priory now is a symbol of all that is beautiful, permanent, enduring, in the life of Cartmel.

The Cartmel coast is so pleasant, the climate so kind, it has become increasingly desirable as a place for retirement. Those who have loved the Lakes all their lives come to live here, at the gates of their Elysium. Apart from hundreds of new estates little has changed along Morecambe Bay shores, but folk are always apprehensive. They have had the recurring worry of Water Authorities wishing to take Windermere's surplus to impound it in a flooded Winster valley, the proposed barrage across the Kent estuary and constant interference with the "dreaming shores where Kent and Leven roll their waters to the tide".

As one scheme is shelved others take its place. But the protectionists and nature lovers forge ahead. The Nature Trails are excellent projects, and there are plans to make of the Kent estuary, including Arnside and Silverdale, a new country park.

The Vale of Cartmel and Cartmel "town" grow in beauty.

III

"MOST BEAUTIFUL ROAD" NORTH INTO LAKELAND

Through the Vale of Cartmel to Newby Bridge

Windermere Lakeshore highway—from Newby Bridge to Bowness and Ambleside

Some Westmorland dales—Troutbeck valley, Stockdale, by the Brathay and Rothay

Ambleside, Rydal and Grasmere

Over The Raise to Thirlmere and Keswick

Keswick and its neighbouring dales

CARTMEL TO WINDERMERE FOOT

NORTH of Cartmel is a valley, green and gentle, little known and rarely in the news, watered by the River Eea—the name itself means "water"—and its main feeder, Ayside Pool, which begins in a very small lakelet, hardly bigger than a pond, Ayside Tarn. Two centuries ago the vale was marshy, undrained land, a chain of mosses and pools, with a few clustering hamlets on slopes slightly raised above flood level which had started as priory granges and vaccaries, and a few larger farms and houses with histories coeval with that of the Priory. There were footways and bridle-ways along the valley to link the communities with Cartmel and Kendal, difficult and often dangerous, skirting the mosses and crossing unenclosed commons. To-day I sometimes think travel in the Vale of Cartmel would be simpler if there were fewer lanes. Never was there a region with so many four and three lane ends—and so few signposts. Strangers have been known to travel in circles and arrive back bewildered at their starting-points. To make exploration easier let it be known that from Cartmel in a northerly direction are at least six routes all delivering the road-user at Newby Bridge—in their own good time.

Taking these lanes anti-clockwise the most easterly one goes past Longlands and Broughton Lodge estates, and, rounding the northern end of Hampsfell, climbs Old Town Hill into Cartmel Lane and the main highroad at Nether Newton. From Four Lanes End on this route, on St. Andrew's Moor, a pleasant Green Lane climbs steadily to High Newton; at the cross-roads, built into the field wall, is the Egg Pudding Stone, an ovoid, greenstone boulder at which every child looks with a speculative eye, for every one has been told that when the stone hears the Priory clock strike twelve it gets up and turns over in its bed. A perfectly true observation! A third route passes Field Broughton, its church tower an excellent landmark, for it rears its head as proudly as the Priory's. Field Broughton is a very scattered hamlet, its houses standing alongside narrow, twisty by-lanes which in turn send out branches to join the Newby Bridge highway near High Newton or half a mile onwards at Ayside. A fourth route forks from the third—the buses ply along this way, taking summer visitors from Cartmel to Windermere or Ulverston—running through delightful woodlands near Seatle Farm and Fiddler Hall, so into the same highroad little more than a mile from Newby Bridge.

If I should tire of these excellent lanes, made by the 1796 and 1800 highway surveyors, I still have "unimproved lanes", grass-grown and half hidden under brambles and foxgloves and campanulas—paths leading to some Sleeping Palace—or paths climbing to the limestone slopes of Hampsfell, or to the tawny, bracken-clad fells or coppices across the valley. An exhilarating switchback road goes from Cartmel to Wood Broughton and over Bigland Heights, Brow Edge and on the Backbarrow road to Newby Bridge—a road through such beautiful hill-country and overlooking such dramatic distances no traveller bound for the Lakes should miss it.

Of the old halls in the valley Aynsome is one of the oldest—the Eea's holm—built by the Marshalls, who claimed descent from the great William le Mareshal, Earl of Pembroke, who founded the Priory, who was "governor of his King and Kingdom" and gave to the brethren the great estates bestowed upon him by a grateful sovereign. Near the Hall the Eea used to turn the great wheel of the Priory corn mill, to which tenants were compelled to bring all their corn to be ground, paying the dues to the miller in charge. The Marshalls were at Aynsome till two hundred years ago when the Machells, ironfounders of Backbarrow, came here. In their days the Mill Farm had its brewery, with the coachman as head brewer, "one of the best in Cartmel Vale". Twice a year he officiated at great brewings—at the beginning of April, when table ales were brewed, and in October, when strong beer was brewed and put in casks—no water in this heady liquor—to be kept two more years before tapping for Christmas cheer. After the Machells had lived here nearly a century the hall passed to the Remingtons, nephews, who lived at the fine eighteenth-century Longlands Hall, not far away; one a wealthy Ulverston lawyer, another the "restoration" Vicar of Cartmel, a great lover of the open air, and so confirmed an early riser that every morning, winter and summer alike, he climbed to the top of Hampsfell before breakfast. This climb and the world as he saw it from the summit were a constant inspiration to him. He was the builder of the Hospice, from which thousands have also seen the "wonder of the world and all its colours, light and shade".

The early Marshalls of Aynsome had as neighbours the Thornburghs of Hampsfield Hall, powerful free tenants in the valley. Their hall stood beneath the wooded steeps of Hampsfell, a venerable homestead with an old pele a little behind it, a tower where

HAMPSFIELD HALL

the family dependants could find refuge when Scots came near. The ruin was pulled down by a tenant a century ago for the sake of its stones, which he built into his farm. Only the site is marked on large-scale maps. A new Hampsfield was built in the seventeenth century by William Thornburgh, the last male in direct line, after whom the Rawlinsons of Cark Hall bought it. William's mother was Thomasin, one of Sir Robert Bellingham's three heiress daughters from Burneside, who held lands in the Kent valley and at Poulton, a woman of property and a "man of business", as her account books show. His wife has a lengthy versified epitaph in Cartmel church:

"Here before lyeth interred
Etheldred Thornburgh corps in dust
In lyfe at death still firmly fixed
On God to rest hir stedfast trust
Hir father Justice Carus was
Hir mother Katherine his wiffe
Hir husband William Thornburgh was
Whylst here she ledd this mortall lyfe——"

From the hall rough sheep-tracks and grassy loanings climb to the fell. From one of them we can see two stones—Robin Hood and Little John, though the two outlaws bold can have no remote connection with Cartmel—waymarks, or shepherds' gathering stones, placed there centuries ago.

I have pleasant memories of the quiet Sunday afternoon when I made my sketch of the Hall. I descended upon it from the thyme-scented heights of the fell, not far north of the boulders Robin Hood and Little John, which are in a direct line with the house and farm, though hundreds of feet nearer the sky. A field path went down to the fell foot, into a green lane where campanula, scabious and meadow crane's-bill grew in profusion, and hedgerow honeysuckle and the sweet short clover of nearby fields most deliciously scented the air.

What I saw of the front of the hall my picture shows. From the rear it looks even more interesting, but I talked so long with Mr. Crowe, the farmer, in the field behind the house, I made no second sketch. On the slope where we stood grass-grown mounds and ridges showed where had been the site of the first Hall of the fourteenth century. "There's the foundation of a castle," said Mr. Crowe, pointing to a mound higher than the rest, probably where stood the pele. It must have been a fine place of outlook, watching the Vale of Cartmel and the approaches from the Bay. To the pele hurried the terrified folk of the Vale when rumours came of raiders seen crossing the Leven or Duddon Sands.

Inside the Hall Mrs. Crowe and her daughters did the honours, showing me the carving, W.T.M. 1687, on a spice cupboard inside the old fireplace—with a grated window near it where a farm boy sat reading the Sunday paper, looking up occasionally to watch the world pass by. But nothing moved. They showed me the dark attics covering five bays over the west and oldest part of the house, the timbers all wooden-pegged, and, at the south end, the huge, stone chimney stack built within the gable end of the attic. But they did not know how a large stone came to be carved with the head of a thick-lipped Negro, though I later learned of a Crowe who captained a Slaver in the 1800's. One room had recesses deep within the walls where cheeses used to stand—and now came recollections of earlier generations at the hall who practised a different type of farming.

They do not make cheeses in Cartmel now, nor is lime burning a local industry. Mr. Crowe, however, remembers the lime kiln behind the hall being in use about 1900, the last to be fired in Cartmel.

"When we were lads, on off days we were sent up fell for loads of stone—Hampsfell is nothing but limestone. We carted it down and over a few years we collected a tidy heap. Then we were sent to Grange gas works for coke. Then we were ready for stoking up. The kiln was kept burning ten days or so, and at the end of it we had enough lime to last us four years. We used to sell some to pay for the coke."

He told me also of days when the lads used to go over Bigland or Howbarrow to Holker Mosses to cut peats, and of an old uncle who was prevailed upon to use new mechanical aids on the farm.

There was a new hay machine at Hampsfield, the first he had seen, a scatterer and turner. The old man thought his fork would do the job better and he ordered the farm lad to bring his fork, too, and work with him. By the time the two of them had turned one row the machine had finished the field. The man mopped his brow. "Come on, lad," he said. "Thee and I might as weel gan yam." He was won over.

The next mansion updale is Broughton Lodge, known as St. Andrew's Moor in the eighteenth century when Mr. Stockdale's grandparents lived there. When news of Jacobite rebels coming into Westmorland reached them they sent their daughters away into the remoter hills for safety, but the next year, in 1746, Mrs. Stockdale was away to London, riding pillion behind her husband, returning to tell her family of the sights she had seen—pikes bearing the heads of executed rebels at Manchester and the rows of rebels' heads of high degree impaled on Temple Bar, one of the grisly relics being the head of Captain Fletcher, related to the Stockdales.

Across the valley at Wood Broughton lived the Knypes, who were free tenants of the Priory, and near by is Townson Hill, where as a boy young Robert Mackereth was in service. His master had him educated; later he found work as a waiter in

London, became friendly with another waiter with big ideas, who planned with him to go to India to find their fortunes. Robert certainly did, for twenty years later he was back in Cartmel, was knighted for his services, and from his great wealth saw that those of his relations who were in need should be helped. A sister Mary, a simple creature, was given an annuity; it was payable in Kendal, so over the fells she used to walk to claim it.

On the west side of the river and not far from the lane served by the bus are High Cark Hall, a fine old farm, and Seatle, a

HIGH CARK HALL FARM

little community at a "dead end", a peaceful backwater where swallows swoop over stooks of golden corn on August evenings, wood pigeons croon drowsily from deep copses and warm scents drift in the breeze from the flowers in the gardens fronting tall house and lowly cottage. The high fells, the Allotments of each farm, rise behind them, criss-crossed by old tracks which are fine walking, over to Bigland or Backbarrow. In spring the in-pastures are full of young lambs and the floors of the plantations are carpeted with flowers; in autumn, landscapes superb greet one on the skyline. Lakeland is not far away over the top of these fells. From High Brow Edge the scene is overwhelming.

The cottagers realize its beauty and, so that a stranger might enjoy it the more, reel out the names of mountain and fell.

Across the valley are three more retiring hamlets, each with charm, the atmosphere of antiquity and no pretensions to any fame whatever; as far as I know Field Broughton, Barber Green and Ayside have all kept out of history books, the news and modern guides. They must have been here in monastic times as communities of priory herders. After the dissolution the lands passed into laymen's hands. Flowery lanes run away behind

SEVEN YEWS FARM—BARBER GREEN

Field Broughton church or beyond Field Broughton hamlet to Egg Pudding Stone corner on St. Andrew's Moor—the chapel of that name has long disappeared. No one remembers the Cartmel Races which were formerly held here, but the stone is still here. More narrow lanes, where you surprise a hare nibbling at the hedgeside, or a squirrel nutting in October, go north to Head House, where there are caves in the limestone scars and relics of the days when limestones from the quarries were taken away to the coast. When you least expect it you come upon the hamlet of Barber Green, which advertises its existence on only one guide stone, a beautifully lettered stone carved by eighteenth-century road-makers.

Here are pleasant cottages, a Georgian house, and the farm with the Seven Yews, the subject of my sketch, a typical Cartmel farm of post-monastic days.

Seven Yews Farm has low, heavy-raftered rooms, a fireplace into which one of the cumbrous carts in the yard could have been driven with room to spare, and a finely carved court cupboard built into the thickness of the wall, its date 1630.

This hamlet has its girdle of great trees, much loved by singing birds, a small grass plot for a central green not much used by the animal population because here they assume the road was made for them; ducks, geese, turkey chicks and guinea fowl disport themselves on the Queen's highway, farm dogs fall asleep thereon and refuse to give right of way to any misguided human who strays upon it. The postman's van and an occasional tradesman are the only regulars—and an old, retired farmer who cycles slowly by, night and morning, milk pail over the handlebars, to milk his one cow in a field near the cross-roads. Life is very pleasant and very peaceful here, but my days are never long enough. Always before going to bed I climb to the brow top to see a sight which can never pall; it may be the spill of sunset colour over the eastern fells which throws mountain peaks into purple relief, throws flames across emerald pools of sky, turning all the old grey farms to pale pink and lilac; or it may be the sight of Lakeland drawing down its fleecy white blanket of mist, or again the moonlight may be silvering the valley and glinting on the fells above Windermere, with black pikes cutting into the sky above Langdale. When the hamlet lies asleep under the quiet sky the loudest noise comes from a cow tearing sweet grass from her dew-wet pasture, or an owl hunting over the yews, or one of the farm guinea fowl acting watch-dog for us all.

Folk remember two local characters of twenty years ago. One is Billy Hent; the other, Swainson of the Smithy. The former is a leathery little man who dresses in queer and outmoded style, a shapeless old hat, tight drain-pipe trousers, a short "brat", he is seen striding along the lanes with a sack over his shoulders or some burden on his arm. I think I shall overtake him and I shall see him face to face, but no, his effortless strides carry him round a corner and he is gone. His home is an upturned boat near the inn of a nearby village. When road authorities moved the cottage and his boat for road works he disappeared into the hills. But back he came to continue his old way of life; he cooks, patches and mends his clothes, is an excellent stone-waller and takes nothing as a gift. When the villagers, knowing he must be well over pensionable age, persuaded him to apply for what he was entitled to, said he: "They'll not give me summat for nowt?" He objected, but finally was induced to take the money. Soon afterwards he began to be "bothered wi' his feet". "It's that money brought this on. I knew it were wrong. No man's meant to get summat for nowt." What independence he has always shown! He once built a good wall for an employer, but when his pay was owed to him overlong he pulled down the wall and left it at that. His sort have always found a niche in village life;

QUIET CORNER—NEWTON-IN-CARTMEL

Cartmel has an affection for its old "characters". Another ancient who refused to retire was a Broughton blacksmith—eighty-six and still going strong when I first saw him at his smithy at the roadside. A burly young farmer had just brought in a powerful impatient cart-horse to be shod, a huge creature which seemed capable of demolishing the old smithy with one blow of a great hoof. It was no easy task but the old man would not confess himself beaten. The farmer cajoled and threatened the animal as it reared, plunged and backed, but the blacksmith held on like grim death, his language, enriched by the experience of a long life, flowing in full spate.

If anyone in the hamlet feels the need for noise and bustle all he or she has to do is to climb the hill—and there is the busy highway, a great, wide road which had to demolish part of Lindale and cut through the heart of High Newton to satisfy the need for speed. It is a road much too wide and too many of its corners have been cut off, but the road-makers seem to be proud of their achievement. Heavy traffic bound for Barrow, Millom and Whitehaven comes this way to avoid the narrow hilly streets of Allithwaite, Flookburgh or Holker; thousands of motor-coaches

VALE OF CARTMEL HAMLET—AYSIDE

pass through "to the Lakes". Like Lindale, High Newton has its quiet corners, the post office-cum grocers behind a yew tree, low, old cottages with heavy beams darkening the rooms, and geraniums in the windows, a fine old house with a dated doorway, little backwaters with creeper-covered barns jutting out at awkward angles. One house was a former inn, the Horse and Farrier, but to-day the only inn is the brightly painted Crown across the broad highway. George Fox came to Newton-in-Cartmel on his first journey through Lancashire, coming from Underbarrow and Crosthwaite over the Westmorland border to the house of one James Taylor.

High Newton spelled comparative comfort to wayworn travellers who had crossed Tow Top, and its inns must have been a cheerful sight to many in the days of uneasy travelling.

High Newton watches the Lakewards tourist pass by. But to see the third of the trio of ancient hamlets I mentioned one must turn a little from the main highway—or along byways from Barber Green—to find Ayside with its scattered farms and a narrow bottle-neck which seems to say "full stop" to road users in unseemly haste. It is a flower-embowered place, smothered in roses, honeysuckle, and creepers. There is a scent of Sweet Cecily on the summer air and a pervading accompaniment of bird song. My sketch I made one summer evening.

In discovering these hamlets the traveller comes upon the real old-world Cartmel, which has changed but little in the essential things. Most strangers, however, will be content to leave them undiscovered as they make northwards to Newby Bridge.

NEWBY BRIDGE AND LEVEN FORDS

Newby Bridge, a place of high antiquity, was of early importance in the road systems of Lakeland because of the fords of the River Leven, which empties Windermere at its southern outlet. It was on the line of the busy highway linking Kendal and Ulverston markets—a road we have already seen from Gummers How and Scout Scar, which dropped from the fell, at Fell Foot, to two fords which offered short cuts. Both fords were lost with the deepening of the channels for the coming of the lake steamer service in 1845.

Old writers tell of a stone called the Cheesepress which showed above water-level when the ford was safe and which also marked the position of a deep pit called Bass Hole. Shallow draught barges from the Langdale end of the lake, bringing slates downstream to be unloaded on to wagons at the landings used to reload with lime brought from the old kilns still to be seen in the Vale of Cartmel; there were quarries and kilns along the edge of Hampsfell and behind Head House Hill, near Hampsfield Hall and Longlands. The barges often found the rocks in midchannel difficult to avoid; when they returned with loads of lime to the lake head they threw lumps of it overboard into the shallow water to show the best passage between the submerged boulders. After the coming of the first steamers the offending rocks were hauled with great difficulty—some were a ton weight and over—

out of the channel and deposited on the shore just below Landing How.

Both fords lay between Newby Bridge and the rounded peninsula opposite Fell Foot and the brow down which comes the old road from Kendal. The upper ford joined the lakeshore at Fell Foot with Landing How, the crossing, because of the peninsula, being narrowed to fifty-five yards, the depth, when the Cheese-press showed, being under three feet. The lower ford, half a mile above Newby Bridge, was eighty yards wide but averaged two feet in depth—perfectly safe if you kept away from the " unfathomable " Dog Hole, and did not get stuck fast in the mud, like the unfortunate tinker who drowned there, in an upright position, pack on back—a tragedy from which, it was said, Tinkler's Ford took its name.

Quite frequently in the old days, as now, there were periods when no travellers could look at the Leven waters without shuddering; after heavy rains the river in spate is a terrible sight to see and the roll-back flood-waters, carrying torn-up trees and dead sheep, seem to threaten the very masonry of the old bridge. The Leven has within it the combined waters of Rothay, Brathay, rivers from Colwith, Skelwith and Langdale, from Stockgill and Scandale, from Troutbeck, from Esthwaite Water and Cunsey—each in flood can be a terrible thing, but together the waters after storms make man and the works of man look very little and puny.

The happiest time to visit Newby Bridge is on a sunny summer day when children in gay frocks bend to the water to throw bread to the swans and a kingfisher flashes above the Mill Race by the venerable Corn Mill.

WATER MILL AND EEL TRAPS

What do you know about eels? I must confess that until recently I knew very little. They wriggled; they often came out of the Ribble on a fisherman's hook instead of the trout he hoped for. When a child wriggles like an eel we say " he's as wick as a snig ". East End Londoners have a liking for jellied eels whereas northerners show a preference for tripe. Eels have a very well-developed wanderlust; when the biological urge comes for them to travel, off they wriggle down drain, gutter and river to the open sea and then it is non-stop to the Saragossa Sea where they breed in such great numbers the Atlantic Ocean is " wick wi' 'em ".

And that was the sum total of what I knew about eels.

But one day near Newby Bridge I actually met an eel catcher. I saw an eel trap and a wriggling, squirming, Laocoon-like mass of potential jellied eels, when I least expected to find anything of the sort.

When I was staying with Miss B. she remarked one day, "I think you ought to call on the two old corn millers. They'll be able to tell you a lot you want to know."

People always take for granted my "insatiable curiosity" and direct me to friends and relations who are knowledgeable on the

OLD CORN MILL—NEWBY BRIDGE

widest variety of subjects—which all makes life extremely interesting.

I went to the Corn Mill, a most romantic-looking old building which fitted in so perfectly with its setting of oak, alder and hazel coppice that though I had passed along the nearby highway many times I had never guessed at its existence. Its aged stones were mantled with creepers, every cranny had its tiny plants. Tacked on to the mill was the prettiest little miller's cottage with a porch hung with purple velvet clematis and tea roses round the windows. The step by the garden gate was half a nether millstone. Worn millstones were incorporated in the pavings of the garden path and more of them had been utilized to span an unused water-channel.

"Uncle Tom" and "Uncle Harry" were septuagenarians, both quiet-voiced old men who whiled away a rainy hour by showing me first the mill (Uncle Tom's sphere) and then the out-door "works".

Never have I seen a building more like a fortress; many of the border peles have walls less heavy and they were designed for defence.

"Aye, it's been standing a good few years I dare say. Five hundred years likely—sin' t' day o' t' monks. Look you—somebody cut that date up there—1617, isn't it?" So it was, a date carved deep in an oaken beam over the door. Early nineteenth-century dates were painted on plaster—and early twentieth-century calculations were scribbled on posts and doors. How well the old mill bridges the centuries! Mills have changed little in the thousand years in which man has diverted waters to turn his mill wheels; I could in the modern gear recognize the same workings I had seen in drawings of mediæval mills. The mill race diverted from the rushing river turned the same type of ponderous wheel (here the undercut type of iron plate wheel —not buckets) and this turned within the building a wooden cog wheel with wooden teeth which, in turn, caused the grindstones on the floor above to rotate. As in the primitive mills the meal passed into hoppers and so was piled into sacks to be carried away.

Everywhere was a coat of white meal—dustings of it on ledges, piles in corners and a muffling carpet on the floors. Most free from the dust was the perforated tiled floor of the chamber where years ago oats were roasted. Below was the vaulted kiln—but no fire has been lit there for many years.

"Once on a day every local farmer brought his own oats here to be ground and kept himself supplied with his own oatmeal." The old man sighed. Milling stopped some years ago.

"There was nowt like it," he added. "And nowt like stone-ground whole meal for bread."

We descended worn stairs—a rope for handrail—crossed the ground floor—completely paved with worn and broken grindstones—and stood by the door to watch the sunlit silver rain fall.

It was then I noticed the doorway and how two blocks of wood had been built into the stone masonry on each side. They were more pitted with holes than a much-used dart board, some holes held rusted nails and on some nails were scraps of skin.

"Oh, that? That's where we skin eels—and where they've

been skinning 'em as long as theer's bin a miller living here." He satisfied my curiosity. Eels: to kill and skin. First you break its back, then you knock a nail through it to the wooden door frame, and neatly with pincers skin it.

"And if anyone's got a sprained wrist an eel skin clapped on is best cure."

"But first you catch your eel," said I. "Easy," said Uncle Tom, and at once hailed brother Harry. The rain was over. Over rain-wet stones spanning the mill stream, through wet grass by the still water (the mill wheel was not turning to-day) Uncle Harry led me until we reached a little sluice gate under which a few inches of water ran—down a wooden-floored slide into a large wooden box.

"There's your eels—trapped. There's no escape for 'em."

And there they were, wriggling in their watery prison, a score or so, slim, foot long squirmers to a giant of an eel over a yard long which would sell for a good price in Manchester, at 1s. 6d. a pound.

"Season's just beginning in August. Night brings the eels down—they come out of the lake into the river, down our mill stream and—there's our traps waiting for 'em. Easy!"

Eel catching has always been a sideline for corn millers on our northern rivers. I could imagine the miller of mediæval times eyeing with approval the catch of a summer night as he despatched them to the prior of Cartmel, his master.

The two brothers, being members of an old Newby Bridge family, were just the men to tell me of the old days and to recall traditions of the place. Not only had Knowles for several generations been millers, but Knowles had also been landlords of the Swan, in the days which saw the passing of the coaching era and the coming of the Furness Railway. They ran the last mail coaches which plied from Ulverston and it was interesting to learn of a local version of the Rowland Hill penny post story which I had always associated with Buttermere. Newby Bridge natives like to think that it was whilst staying at the Swan, Sir Rowland had the idea of cheap postage; a servant girl at the inn had to refuse a letter from her sweetheart for lack of money for the postage. Maybe earlier he had also seen a poor Buttermere lass bound to refuse a letter from her brother though she confessed she knew the chief item of news in it—a cross on the outside told her "he was coming home soon". A century ago the Swan entertained a never-ending flow of "lions"; visitors included Charlotte Brontë and Nathaniel Hawthorne. How ready for refreshment the wayfarers of old must have been when they saw its hospitable door open! Where there were busy fords, and a bridge, and later boat-landings, and a railway terminus, the inn was most important. So was the old smithy near by, for until a century ago most travellers came on horseback. Nowadays road-users are more likely to look out for one of the motor association's road patrols who often stands at the very busy corner.

LAKESIDE ROAD—NEWBY BRIDGE TO BOWNESS BAY

Wordsworth in his Guide writes that the "lower part of the lake is rarely visited but has many interesting points of view, especially at Storrs Hall and at Fell Foot". No longer is the first part of this statement true, but near the road are places little visited: the village of Staveley, for instance—Staveley-in-Cartmel to distinguish it from another, Staveley-in-Kendal. Staveley is a common name meaning "place where staves were cut". It is a quiet spot, isolated on a by-lane, with white walls peeping between dark yew trees, and coppices clothing the fells behind it. The cottagers are fond of rose bowers and clematis over the porches; in their sheltered coign they keep summer's flowers well into November. Beyond the clustered houses the lane wanders to the tiny village school and the church—with memories of Edmund Law the schoolmaster-parson who walked daily for nearly forty years from Buck Crag, near Lindale, to serve his parishioners here. Memories of a clergyman who preceded him are vivid too, the "Priest" Camelford, who angered George Fox so deeply when he came to this "chapell" in 1652.

His visit he records with some detail in his diary—how after Camelford had done preaching he, Fox, "began to speak the word of life to him and Camelford was in such a rage and a fret and so peevish that he had not patience to hear, but stirred up the rude multitude", who hauled him out of the church, struck and punched him and the church-warden, John Knipe, threw him headlong over the wall. Fox is pleased to record that Knipe "ye Lorde after cutt off", and the youth "writing after the priest", John Braithewaite, was "convinct" and later became a minister of the Gospel. From Fox's writing and his wife's letters condemning Camelford—"If ye own Camelford ye must deny God"—we might think the minister was not fit for his cloth, but among his own sect—he was a Presbyterian—he was spoken of as "a useful preacher in this remote corner" and a "godly and painful man".

Staveley church has been rebuilt; only memories remain of Fox, Camelford and Law, and of the good lady of Fell Foot who was ever mindful of the poor in the parish. She was a daughter of the designer and builder of Eddystone lighthouse, married Mr. Dixon who built the mansion, and devoted herself to "good works". The nearest doctor was over in Kendal or at Cartmel, so when folk were ill they came to her to be bled, or vaccinated, or for medicine from her own supply of "simples". There was no form of education for the poor girls of the parish so she built a school and endowed it. When the corpse of a Staveley person was taken to Cartmel, the nearest burial place, it had to be carried by relays of bearers, so she provided a hearse. When she herself died she left £200 to the poor. Before her husband built Fell Foot the Robinsons had lived at the older house—two brothers who "never spoke without swearing", earning the nicknames of "Black Jack and Terrible Dick".

The wooded country along the lake shore to Bowness mercifully screens the caravan site from Fell Foot northwards; we cannot always see the lake for the trees. Much is coppice country, but less so than formerly, when coppice wood was grown and felled at fifteen yearly intervals to be used for charcoal. Old pictures of the lake shore show the pyramidical stacks of wood tended by charcoal burners and blue spires of smoke rising against the flame and gold of birch and oak—to be used in the bloomeries of Furness. Coppice wood was also grown for the swill makers, who plaited baskets of oak spales and hazel—such as we could often see being made in the rear premises of cottages at Backbarrow, for the bobbin mills, which still are in existence, one being across the lake at Stott Park; and for the stripping of oak bark for tanning. In the eighteenth century some of the woodcutters at Blakeholme Wray made use of a stone hut which stood deserted near the lake shore. They called it Cornelius Shop and believed that it had been built as a hide by a fugitive from justice who lived a hermit-like life here. The hut is still there and from a local workman I heard of the owner's—Sir John Fisher—insistence that in doing alterations Cornelius Shop should not be touched. The local tradition hints that Cornelius was a Spaniard, survivor from the storm-driven Armada, who came ashore at Maryport and sought refuge inland. A dark-skinned Spanish family, they say, was once living in these parts, descendants of the said Cornelius.

Lake-shore woodmen stored up such tales. They had legends of buried silver deep within the lake near Ladyholm and Silverholm, they talked of wraiths and water kelpies howling before approaching storm, of the Catcrag boggle—or boggart, and doubtless looked for the white ghost which was said to wail above the heights of Claife overlooking the Ferry. Long ago, they said, on a wild and stormy night the ferryman heard a shout for the boat from Ferry Nab and went out, to obey the summons—but found no one. He returned dumb with fear. Soon afterwards he died, telling no one of what he had seen. Later the crying for the ferry was repeated on the stormiest nights, a cry which struck so much terror into the hearts of the lakeside folk that they called for a monk from Furness to exorcize the unquiet spirit. In a quarry near the ferry he was "laid for ever". When such tales were repeated the woodcutters tending their fires would tell another story of tragedy at the Ferry. There was a wedding, they said, and all the wedding guests returned over the lake full of jest and jollity, laughter and singing sounding along the water. Half-way over, the boat sank and all, forty-seven, were drowned. That was in the autumn of 1653.

Another local tradition is linked with the fine late Georgian mansion called Storrs which lies in lovely gardens on the left of our road. "They used to keep slaves tied up in the cellars", I was once told. The slave trade linked with Lakeland? It is true William Wilberforce lived once at Rayrigg, a few miles north from Storrs, and that black servants were not uncommon—the Stockdales had them at Cark and negroes were employed at Graythwaite Hall over the lake.

A number of famous names are associated with Storrs. Near this spot the artist, Constable, watching the beauty of great clouds moving across the mountains, was deeply moved and inspired to fix upon paper that fleeting loveliness. Years later, when the Boltons were living at Storrs, Sir Walter Scott was fêted and honoured on his birthday by one of the most colourful lake "pageants" of the century. Canning was a guest at Storrs, and Scott and his daughter, and Lockhart, his biographer, stayed at Elleray with "Christopher North"—Professor Wilson, who was often dubbed, because of his interest in Windermere sports and regattas, "Lord High Admiral of the Lakes". He was prime mover in the Lake District Sports and Regattas held at the Ferry, when wrestling and running were indulged in as well as aquatic sports. But in August 1825 he arranged the most lavish spectacles—which Lockhart records in his *Life of Scott*—

"Brilliant cavalcades in the woods in the mornings, delicious boatings on the lake by moonlight . . . and one of the most splendid regattas that ever enlivened Windermere . . . not fewer than fifty barges following in the Professor's radiant procession when it paused at the Point of Storrs". Here they took on board the Boltons and their guests, and "The Bards of the Lakes", including Wordsworth and Southey, "called for three cheers for Scott and Canning".

The nomenclature of the Windermere region is full of interest. Although the word "holm" in other parts of the north means low-lying fields by rivers, here the holms are the islands so beautifully set upon the bosom of the lake. Blake Holme, Silver Holme, Grass Holme, Ling Holme and Ramps Holme lie between the lake-foot and the Ferry and northwards are delightful islets named after the Lilies of the Valley, the Crow, the Snake, the Maiden—and Lady Holme, upon which once stood a chapel to the Virgin Mary, an enchanted place in which William Wilberforce used to delight, rowing there from Rayrigg, his house, early in the morning. The headlands jutting out into the lake on which we can stand and feel almost as though we were on the lake itself, with wavelets lapping on either hand—and swans coming up to us, hopeful for food, are in local speech "nabs". In his Guide, Father West often took his "station" on lakeside nabs, there to survey the scene—and how he lavished his praise on landscapes "which beggared description"! Like many of the early topographers he placed this lake high in the list for the most beautiful. "Arthur Young", he wrote, "gave preference to Windermere"; Mr. Pennant "compares it to the chief of the Scotch lakes and concludes it to be here what Lomond is there". He approved of its trim appearance—Mrs. Linton's "mountain child with its Sunday frock on"—for there was nothing untidy on the margin, "not one bulrush or swampy reed defiles the margin of this imperial lake. No lake has its border so well ascertained and of such easy access. Not one, after Lomond, can boast of so vast a guard of mountains with such variety and diversity of shore."

This praise from so many pens West hoped would not deter the tourist in his journey northwards. "This ought not to prejudice the minds of those who have the Tour to make, against such as prefer Derwentwater or Ullswater. The styles are all different——"

In 1844 the author of the *Pictorial History of Lancashire* let himself go in describing the road from Newby Bridge to the

Ferry—the "rich emerald-hued meadows reflected in cerulean waters, sweetly rounded coves and fairy bays, coppice-clothed eminences wildly beautiful—ever new and varying, the lakeside road kept curiosity constantly alert in expectation of what the next opening would reveal". Nearing the Ferry he experienced one of those tantalizing weather changes which do their part in adding to Lakeland's infinite variety. He came to the "little causeway consisting of a few loose stones—so near the ferry-house on the other shore that if the boat should not be on the Bowness side one will put off for his conveyance". No clockwork time-table about the ferry a century ago. At the ferry-house inn, "so beautifully situated", he and his companion sought refreshment and seeing a house so handsomely furnished they hugged themselves on their good luck. But the food was a sad let down; "a bit of poor bacon, three fingers in width, a heaped-up plate of rusks of thin oats resembling bits of chamois-leather stiffened in glue——" So, much annoyed, they set off for Hawkshead, after one glance at the twilit lake, "tranquil and glossy", and Curwen's Island, known as Belle Isle to-day.

Let us leave the disgruntled travellers to wend their way to Hawkshead. We have no associations but pleasant ones in our memories of the Ferry and the hotel. The very first meal I ever ate in Lakeland, as a very impressionable schoolgirl, was tea on the lawn of the Ferry Hotel. What I ate apart from coffee walnut cake I cannot recall, but doubtless it was all nectar and ambrosia to me. Mention the Ferry and I bring to mind swans lurking hopefully near the shore for food to be thrown to them, the lovely sight of yachts skimming lightly like birds—beautiful enough to put even the swans out of countenance—with white, orange and red sails bellying in the breeze—the passing of the launches and the pleasure boats laden with trippers. Pleasant are all of these to recall, and the saunter along the path to Bowness Bay, a walk now made free for us, through lands owned by the National Trust skirting the edge of Parsonage Bay, to Cockshott Point and the boat-building sheds and boat-houses, to the bus stands and motor parks, the queues and crowds at Bowness Pier. Modern tourism takes over.

Windermere for centuries has been a place with boating memories. When Mrs. Fiennes came along the narrow and winding lanes from Kendal to Bowness in 1698, what did she do at once? She took a boat out to Belle Isle—"one of great bigness of 50 acres of ground on which is a house—it did not look bigg at the shore, but taking boate I went on it and found it as large and very good barley and oates and grass". Having eaten excellent char fish at Mrs. Rowlandson's at the King's Arms in Kendal, she was curious to see the char in Windermere, which she believed "was the only place that fish is found in". But though the lake was very clear "and full of good fish", the char was out of season and not to be caught, Michaelmas to Christmas being the season for them. Char are still to be caught in the lake and efforts to increase their numbers, as well as of trout, are being made by the Freshwater Biological Association, which carries out its experiments, with Ferry House as headquarters. Tons of pike and perch are trapped each September to keep down their numbers, this being one method of putting up the char population.

A century later who was disporting himself on the "plain of Windermere"? None but the schoolboy Wordsworth.

> "When summer came
> Our pastime was, on bright half-holidays,
> To sweep along the plain of Windermere
> With rival oars——"

directing a course to one or other of the islets, one an island "musical with birds", another "sown with lilies of the valley like a field", a third with the ruins of a shrine "once to Our Lady dedicate". At times the boys frequented an inn "midway on Winander's eastern shore" to seek refreshment; "strawberries and mellow cream were not wanting". Before night fell they returned in their pinnace to the far shore, leaving one of their number, "the minstrel of our troop", on one of the islands, and as they drifted on he played to them upon his flute, seated alone upon a rock:

> "Oh, then the calm
> And dead still water lay upon my mind,
> Even with the weight of pleasure, and the sky
> Never before so beautiful, sank down
> Into my heart, and held me like a dream."

Anyone who has drifted over the bosom of the shadowy lake on a quiet evening has shared the same poignant feelings, and returning has always been full of pleasurable anticipation. Young Wordsworth, a student at Cambridge, could not cover the miles from Kendal to the Ferry too quickly on his return to holiday at Hawkshead, bounding down the last hill, shouting for the ferry as he ran, his cries heard by the "Charon of the Flood", who put out in his boat and drew up at the "jutting pier".

In the early years of the nineteenth century there were many interested witnesses of the newly organized Windermere regattas and sports. These were no elaborate affairs, but merely a succession of boat races, foot races and wrestling, held at the Ferry Inn. The competitors seem to have been the residents along the lake shore, owners of sailing-boats—Bolton, Wilson, Pedder—and Mr. Curwen of Belle Isle, who was so hurt on being beaten in a 1810 regatta that he gave up the contest and decided to sell all his craft. After the boat racing came a kind of amphibian foot race, the course being marked out by stakes in yard-deep water but having deeper pitfalls dug into the lake bed so that the runners would stumble, disappear and then struggle to shallower water, much to the amusement of the onlookers. Miss Weeton, the governess at Doves Nest, describes the affair in a lively manner, and the disgust of all the ladies present when the running-drawers of one of the participants came to grief and every female left the scene. Later in the century regattas became much more spectacular events and now they are colourful highlights of the Windermere "season".

The Mr. Wilson mentioned in the 1810 regatta was John Wilson, better known by his pen name "Christopher North", who came under the spell of Windermere as a student during vacation from Oxford, bought land on Orrest Head and when he came down from college settled at Elleray, eager to enjoy life to the uttermost—swimming, boating, fishing, wrestling and talking with Wordsworth, the Coleridges and de Quincey, who all became friends of his. He was scholar, sportsman and great humorist. A tale of him was told by an old Bowness man to Ashley Abraham, one which shows that even when he became Professor of Moral Philosophy at Edinburgh University he was no less fond of a good joke. One day, seeing two boatmen rather the worse for drink, he called for them to row him across to Wray in their heaviest boat. They willingly complied—everyone sought to please the Professor—and as he lay at ease in the boat bottom they plied the oars vigorously.

After some time one turned round to speak to the Professor. Imagine his horror when he saw no great giant of a man sprawling there. The shock sobered both men. They rowed back to Bowness, sure that he was drowned; facing them was the sad duty of telling Mrs. North at Elleray of the tragedy. They rushed uphill, many mourning villagers with them, and knocked at the door of the Professor's house. Who should answer them but North himself, calm, cool, collected and very much alive, in a suit of dry clothes. The two boatmen gasped, "It's the Professor—or the devil himself!" turned tail and raced back to Bowness, to the laughter of their cronies, and certainly of the "drowned man". He was a powerful swimmer, and to slip quietly overboard whilst they rowed and to swim back to shore was a good sort of joke—and a lesson to turn the boatmen away from tippling when plying for hire.

FROM BOWNESS TO THE LAKE HEAD

To a stranger Bowness and Windermere are as one; they are a long village on both sides of the very long, very steep hill which in a most exasperating way links Windermere Station with Bowness Pier. Of course the railway company was to blame for this confusion. Bowness for centuries was the village by the Bay of Windermere, with shelter for boats, ferries, and refreshment for travellers, a cluster of friendly buildings with a low, unpretentious parish church in its midst. Two miles up the fell slopes was a hamlet of Birthwaite, about which no outsider ever heard. The railway came at last, much to the disgust of Wordsworth and his friends.

> "Is then no nook of English ground secure
> From rash assault?
> Plead for the peace thou beautiful romance
> Of nature, and if human hearts be dead
> Speak, passing winds; ye torrents with your strong
> And constant voice, protest against the wrong!"

The terminus was high flung at Birthwaite. But the tourist was not to be lured into Lakeland by a ticket to Birthwaite; necessity had to name the station Windermere though the lake is a good two miles away. In the last century Windermere of the railway station has grown and little Bowness, too, has grown, and both are to the outsider but one—shops, grey slate-built houses, boarding houses, hotels, cafés, nursery gardens and enchanting views of the lake glimpsed through trees. Relics of the old Bowness lie about the church, and within the fifteenth-century edifice are many ancient and curious features, among them stained glass from Cartmel Priory, upon which can be seen the arms of George Washington's ancestors—mullets and bars, which probably gave the first United States an idea for their flag; Wessingtons and Washingtons were linked with the history of Burneside, Carnforth and Warton, and farms near Shap. The Philipsons, a family we have already met in the Winster valley, and shall meet again at Calgarth Hall, were responsible for a cryptic inscription which, translated from Latin, reads thus—" I am delivered from the jaws of Fawkes. Here is my secret safety." Was Christopher Philipson especially singled out by the plotters, or might he have been killed if the Gunpowder Plot had succeeded?

In July 1840 the widowed Queen Adelaide arrived at a Bowness hotel " to do the Lakes ". It was renamed The Royal in her honour, as was the hotel in Kirkby Lonsdale. She attended evensong at Bowness church, after which a waiting barge conveyed her from the bay to a point farther north known for the exquisite prospects to be obtained. The green knoll at Rayrigg has been known as Queen Adelaide's Hill ever since. A lovely viewpoint it still is. It is best reached from Millerground Bridge and along the banks of Wynlass Beck, a little north of Bowness.

After crossing Millerground Bridge the lakeside road has on the left hand what was the Park of the Philipsons of Calgarth, an ancient and powerful family in the old days, their hall lying not far from the place where Troutbeck flows into the lake. Going back to a remote date we unearth the tale of the Calgarth skulls. Kale-garth was once a kale-yard, or vegetable plot owned by two poor people, Kraster Cook and his wife. The kale-yard was a Naboth's Vineyard to Miles Philipson, who coveted the site for his new hall. He invited the pair to dine at his table, after which he accused them of taking a silver cup—and took good care it was discovered at their home. They were hanged as thieves, and Miles had his kale-yard, not at all troubled by the last curse of Kraster's wife; that was remembered later. " Guard thyself, Miles Philipson; thou thinkest thou hast managed grandly, but that tiny lump of land is the dearest a Philipson has ever bought or stole, for you will never prosper, neither your breed—your schemes will wither, the side you take will lose, Philipsons will own no land, and while Calgarth shall stand we will haunt it night and day. Never will ye be rid of us." The haunting took an unusual form; two skulls made repeated appearances at Calgarth, much to the annoyance of many generations of the family; they were burnt in the fire—but they still appeared; they were ground to white dust—and again they were seen whole. Local folk repeated the words of the curse and believed it had been fulfilled in every part when the Philipsons had departed and Dr. Watson, Bishop of Llandaff, bought their Calgarth estates. He, they said, solemnly "laid" the evil skulls. To-day the story of the skulls is forgotten; for that matter even the Bishop who exorcized them is forgotten. It is only in books referring to the part he played in designing the Lakeland landscape that we come across his name—and in the journal of Miss Weeton, who wrote of him in 1810. In Wales he is written of as the absentee bishop who for thirty years lived in his native Westmorland and, apart from the £1,000 it gave him, took not the least interest in his See.

The bishop was a keen agriculturalist and tree-planter, and if he could have had his way he would have been a great drainer and reclaimer of land from the watery wastes. He actually planned to drain Lake Windermere, "expecting to gain some hundred acres by it", a work practicable but too costly, and one which whilst adding to the estates of the landlords who owned the lake shores would at the same time have destroyed much of the beauty of the lake—and made it no longer attractive to the tourists nor to prospective residents, "which the Bishop perhaps foresaw, realizing that increase of lands would not compensate for the decrease of rents". He did, however, enclose his common land on Skiddaw, building walls over it and starting tree planting on the slopes. The trees which were such a feature at Blea Tarn were of his planting too. A number of his contemporaries did not think his work was improvement on the Lakeland scene —the Wordsworths, who disapproved of "alien trees" such as the vulgar larch, and Miss Weeton, who said of the Skiddaw enclosures that the mountain would "be majestic still, but 'twill be majestic without beauty", and of the afforestation that "I shall scarcely think it being clothed with wood will be any additional ornament to it". If only they had seen the geometric plantations of Skiddaw and Whinlatter of this century, how their great guns would have roared! And as for the Calgarth factory controversy which followed in 1945, how they would have joined cause with the Friends of the Lake District and the C.P.R.E.! During the late war the green glades of Calgarth Park were covered by a great flying-boat factory, hangars and a considerable housing estate for the workers.

From the 1950's wartime eyesores were removed, their sites taken by a school and a modern housing estate. The Sunderland flying-boat base is now the White Cross Bay Caravan Park. The fine Lake District National Park Centre is at Brockholes.

The scenery is changing, the mountains are drawing nearer, but there is still nothing wild or rugged in the foreground. For the next few miles, until we leave Grasmere Vale behind, the landscape is to-day just as Mrs. Linton described it nearly a century ago. She wrote of the Windermere-Grasmere country—" it is all Nature under the tuition of a landscape gardener, smoothed and combed, and daintily trimmed—Wordsworth's mountain child with a perpetual Sunday frock on, and curls newly taken out of paper". This was how Victorian tourists liked their scenery.

They could even refer to examples of poverty seen at the wayside as "becoming". Tourists, from their carriages, smiled condescendingly at "parish paupers sitting hammering at the granite in heaps by the way", where it had been piled when quarried from the road-edge banks. After reading Mrs. Linton's book some of them took the road to the Troutbeck valley to see the "picturesque poverty" displayed there.

TROUTBECK LANES

Three lanes climb from the lakeside road to Troutbeck—called Windermere Troutbeck to distinguish it from what is so erroneously dubbed "John Peel's Troutbeck"—Skiddaw way. There is nothing of tumbledown decay there nowadays; here is the neatest, trimmest, bright and smiling village, gay in pink and buff colour-washed walls and almost smothered in roses and flowering bushes. How different from its 1860 state! Mrs. Linton then realized that changes were imminent. "Pretty, dirty, neglected Troutbeck will be cleaned, schooled, and ornamented and made fit company for ambitious Windermere and respectable Ambleside. It is worth seeing in its dirt and neglect, tumbledown cottages . . . casements patched with rags, and paper . . . its destitution and penury all so grandly enframed that its poverty becomes a charm the more . . . picturesque, wild, dirty, diseased, the prosaic architect and schoolmaster will sweep it away before many years are gone."

The Victorian architects and builders did not completely sweep away the old Troutbeck. Many of the wayside farms are two and three centuries old and on the sites of farms owned by earlier "estates men", who were in turn descended from tenth- and eleventh-century Norse settlers in this isolated dale. Town End, the first house, is safe now in National Trust hands, a treasure-house of seventeenth-century craftsmanship, with a fine barn—with typical sloping ramp, across the road. And this is not the only house which preserves relics of the past. Date tablets, ancient wooden galleries, projecting windows, cylindrical chimneys, and carved " kists ", meal arks, and curiously wrought court cupboards used as interior partition walls, are all to be discovered

TOWN END—TROUTBECK

by the persistent, curious traveller in this dale. There is an inn too, known beyond Westmorland, which once carried a famous sign showing a round rubicund man and a pale cadaverous man.

> " O, mortal man, that liv'st on bread,
> How comes thy nose to be so red?
> Thou silly ass that looks so pale,
> It is by drinking Birkett's ale."

The Mortal Man is an inn of considerable age, much older than the Traveller's Rest on Kirkstone Pass, which was licensed as a place of refreshment in 1840 after some tragic deaths of wayfarers crossing along the mountain road in winter storms. The Mortal Man must have been a welcome sight to travellers coming down Garburn road, from High Street, and from Patterdale.

Little lanes, some so narrow one wheelbarrow could cause a traffic hold-up, converge upon the Mortal Man—Guy Lane and Back Lane drop to Low Gate, Trust Lane and Ing Lane, and Idle Lane comes to Scot Brow and Gallow's Howe, where the Lords of Kendale once hanged out of hand sheep stealers and deer poachers in the hunting park of Troutbeck. This great park, farmed by Mrs. Heelis, Beatrix Potter, with its two thousand acres from the dale and the Tongue to the enchanted points of Frossick, Ill Bell and Thornthwaite Crag, was given by her to the National Trust—with the request that never should the wild creatures she loved so much, the fox, the hare, the otter, be hunted therein.

Troutbeck has for long lived with history. Roman legionaries marched along the dale and disappeared into the cloudwrack over the dale head. Scots raiders came out of the mists and swept southwards when the local stalwarts were unable to stem the tide. In the Tudor days it was said the greatest local scourge of the Scots was Hugh Hird, "the gurt lad of Kentmere"—once a poor "cook lad" who took possession of an empty house in the valley, one which had been forfeit to the Crown and, when a tenant appeared, prevented his entry. For this Hugh had to go to London to answer for his contempt of the Law. In London "he showed off his amazing strength to the King, lifting a beam too heavy for ten local ordinary men, tying two bows and breaking them, and showing how he had driven back Scots raiders unaided". Impressed, the King granted him a boon. And the sturdy Hugh asked for his Troutbeck cot, one field near it for cutting turf, and leave to cut wood in Troutbeck Park. Back home he went. Hird Wood is still on the map—but Hugh killed himself, "they say", rooting up trees at the age of forty-two.

They used to say of Troutbeck:

"There's three hundred brigs i' Troutbeck,
Three hundred bulls,
Three hundred constables,
And many hundred feuls."

Maybe the last line can be taken literally, but as for the others they need explaining. The parish or township was indeed possessed of so many bridges, bulls and constables, for it was divided into three parts, each called a Hundred, and each had to maintain one bridge, one bull and one constable. The grass-floored lane which takes us from Troutbeck village by Robin Lane in a great sweep along the foot of Wansfell, to Holbeck, and Skelgill, is Hundreds Road—and what a road! Windermere and all its lovely frame of wooded slope and bare fell is mapped below, never out of sight until we are in the woods beyond Low Skelgill Farm. Wordsworth once wrote of Kirkstone Pass:

> "Who comes not hither ne'er shall know
> How beautiful the world below."

He spoke the truth and the lines are just as applicable to the landscape viewed from Hundreds Lane or from that surprising "station" Jenkins Crag. These ancient fell lanes and tracks give some of the best walking in Lakeland. Part of their charm lies in the knowledge that they have been in continuous use for so long. Walking along them, whether it is springy turf or rough stones that lie underfoot, you feel removed far out of modern times—and far, far away from the busy highways which are in fact quite near.

We return to the lake side again, by Holbeck Lane or Wain Lane, the former passing Briery Close, a mansion to which the Kay-Shuttleworths came in Victorian days, entertaining many friends.

One guest was Charlotte Brontë, who much enjoyed her drives through the surrounding country, but confessed later in a letter to a friend that she would have loved nothing better than to have been allowed to wander free, on foot. She was one to whom travel on wheels was a poor second best. She was an exception; the joys of pedestrianism were not known to many tourists in Lakeland over a century ago; most of them came on horseback, or in their curricles, or even in their coroneted carriages. Touring the Lakes was something the upper classes indulged in and they did not come on foot. The Wordsworths and their friends were not "usual" people. Among early entries in her diary, Dorothy Wordsworth records the pleasure she had in the praise of some natives near Ambleside who complimented her on her walking; doubtless they thought her rather odd to be on foot. Later, her brothers, feeling she was overtaxing her strength, bought for her a pony, on which she enjoyed many mountain excursions. When the Pedders, in 1810, set out for a picnic on Fairfield, they took carts for the ladies, a pony and an ass, and rode up the Scandale road farther than one at least had a mind for, the ladies screaming and in constant fear of either being overturned or precipitated backwards. Later de Quincey wrote of a ride over Kirkstone with the Wordsworths and his justifiable anxiety when a buxom country girl, who drove them, proceeded to whip up the horses on the downhill stretch, urging them on, for, having no brakes, it was the only way to prevent the cart coming against the cruppers. In 1698 Mrs. Fiennes found that she had to combine walking with riding on the mountain roads; on Kirkstone she noted " those great hills are so full of loose stones and shelves of rocks that it's very unsafe to ride them down ".

To return to the Ambleside road, let me quote a passage from Edmund Bogg, written in 1898, on the pleasures of coach travel before the days of the internal combustion engine.

" Few things will be found more pleasurable in the life of an ordinary mortal than a ride by coach from Keswick to Windermere. Several four-in-hand coaches run the journey daily in the season—drawn by four handsome, clean-bodied, clean-limbed, high-mettled horses, well equipped and well driven. The horn is sounded, all passengers are seated, the driver tightens his reins, we are rattling over the stony street——" That was how our grandparents enjoyed their tour of the Lakes, probably in one of Mr. Brown's coaches, " Late of the Queen's Hotel and Oldest Established Livery and Job Master in Ambleside ".

Eighteenth-century tourists used to pull up at the Low Wood Inn—the hostelry on the right of the highway, possessed of as fine views over Windermere as any. To divert these visitors the innkeeper used to " gratify the curious with those remarkable reverberations of sound which follow the report of a gun ", by firing a cannon. This was a great attraction, and one which the tourists dilated upon when they returned home again. They loved noise, whereas we hanker after quiet. We want no " reverberations " in our ears as we look along the great expanse of water, catching the sunlight on the ripples on summer days, smudged by swift stroking cat's-paws on days of wild weather, On a still day, the blue waters under blue skies and the great mountains of Langdale, dreaming to the north-west, here is a scene cradling peace, " calling home the heart to quietness ".

Just beyond Low Wood, lying below the woods of Jenkins Crag, is Doves Nest, the house where Miss Weeton penned her letters and journal—full of observations on the people around her in the years between 1810 and '16. The inhabitants of Westmorland she described as a handsome race, " the lily and the rose " in every face; the shepherds still kept their primitive simplicity and ignorance though the influx of tourists was having its effect. Thirty years earlier, she said, if a stranger lost his way any householder would give him a welcome reception, his best food and best bed, with no hope of monetary gain; in 1810 the old hospitality was dying out. She watched the farmers making hay—using their hands only for spreading it and using no hayforks for loading or unloading. She saw great quantities of pigs kept on the farms and butter, hams and bacon sent away to market. The farmers seemed to have little desire to improve their land or to lay out their money in this way: a breed of men content with things as they were—and their way of life was satisfying. They lived on their own estates—like the Troutbeck estatesmen—clothed themselves and their families with their own wool, ate oaten and wheaten bread of their own making, and grew enough potatoes to serve their tables, " as well as providing their own butter, milk, eggs, cheese, bacon, hams, mutton, and sometimes veal ".

AMBLESIDE TOWN

Ambleside is in sight, the lake head, the delta of the Brathay which brings the accumulated waters of so many rivers and becks into the lake, the many boat-landings and jetties, and again congregations of folk. As at Bowness Pier, boats and the coming and going of boats, prove an irresistible lure. Piers are lively places—" always something going on "—and attractive to the more gregarious among us. When I come into Ambleside I find myself doing what all the rest of the throng are doing, hankering after food, lingering about the piers, haunting shop windows and searching among picture postcards for favourite views. The last-named occupation has engrossed tourists for a century and a half, though formerly it was a more costly occupation. Picture makers have always found a ready market for their wares, from the eighteenth century, when William Green settled in Ambleside for " reasons of health ", and began to make his collection of many hundreds of coloured and pencil drawings, " all entirely finished while the subject was before him ", charging a shilling admission to his two-room exhibition. According to

Miss Weeton, who knew him well, " he charges excessively high for his water colours—a large size, twenty guineas a pair ". By his sales of pictures he kept his wife, six children, and two servants " in respectable style ". Scores have followed in his footsteps, the artists with their modern studios, the photographers, whose work is more within the reach of trippers, and the sellers of view post-cards, plain, coloured and glossy.

Early travellers knew Ambleside as a market town, the authority to hold a Wednesday market weekly and two fairs yearly, the profits of tollage and piccage to be used to help the poor of the community, being granted in the seventeenth century. Eighteenth-century travellers watched the activities centred round the pillared and galleried market hall and about the Cross, the coming of dales farmers with their produce, the buying and selling of wool and woollen yarn, the latter spun by Ambleside spinsters. The October sheep fair was the most important annual occasion once, the streets thronged with a surging crowd of folk, all mixed up with flocks, the bleating of sheep, the smell of sheep——

AMBLESIDE AND RUSH-BEARING

One lovely summer day we took a lake steamer from Lakeside to Ambleside—return tickets, for given the right kind of day the double water passage and a few hours' stay on land is an admirable way of indulging in semi-idleness. Settling down on seats on the upper deck we prepared to enjoy the scene—one which, as Father West declared, " it would be mere vanity to attempt to describe, for it beggars all description ". Father West, however, had to divert his curious travellers, so he was impelled to give words to the scene, one of " elegant deliciousness ":

> " Strain your imagination to command the idea of so noble an expanse of water, thus gloriously environed, spotted with islands more beautiful than would have issued from the happiest painter. Picture the mountains rearing their majestic heads with native sublimity; the vast rocks boldly projecting their terrible craggy points—enclosures of the most charming verdure in the path of beauty—a ravishing landscape."

A path of beauty—yes; ravishing landscape—yes, but for the rest there is eighteenth-century exaggeration. As always, to the stranger the loveliness of the lake is in its "neuks and nabs", the leafy islets—some no larger than rocky points above water-level just big enough to give foothold to a few brooding gulls, some giving root-hold to a single birch tree, all little enclosed worlds of their own, in the constantly changing character of the shore line, where white farms are scattered above hayfields dipping to the little green bays, where children wave to us from pebbly beaches, and gay boats are putting out from the many boathouses. From the mirror-like tranquillity of the southern

BRIDGE HOUSE—AMBLESIDE

reaches the beauty grows until north of Bowness Bay the dale head mountains begin to rear their heads and a succession of little dales push their way between them.

We loitered at the lake-head landings, then wandered on to the pretty park which runs along the northern shores of Windermere, where the Romans built Borrans fort between the Rothay and the lake, and modern children find exciting playgrounds. We soon realized something was impending. A swarm of children wearing wellingtons and outsize thigh boots came running to the beds of rushes in the shallow marginal bays, splashed into the water and with knives began to hack away at them, all very careful in cutting the longest possible specimens. Their work continued with much earnestness for some time, after which the troop, bearing their burdens, proceeded back to a nearby school. By then we had realized that the Feast of St. Anne—the patron saint of Ambleside—was near and all the preparation for the rush-bearing was in progress.

A few hours later we joined the afternoon crowd along the procession route and saw all Ambleside go by—a happy throng led by youths bearing their burdens—a great harp of rushes, tall spires of seven and eight feet high wreathed in flowers, crosses interwoven with golden bracken and pink clover, crosses of all shapes and sizes, a golden crown on a standard of rushes. The youths bore them proudly, the tallest spires with their plumes of flowers showed above the heads of the crowd far along the route. Then came a helter-skelter of children, tiny tots in rush- and flower-bedecked prams pushed by mammas wearing rather amused, self-conscious smiles, intently serious small boys, burdens gripped in hot hands, beautiful little girls with faces lovelier than the flowers they carried, and behind them more youths and men with larger, heavier bearings.

They all passed by, the music of the local band died away and again could be heard the prattle of Stocks Beck and the voices of half the world. There were two Indian women in brilliant saris near us, a dark East African girl, and a number of Scandinavian youths in walking garb and carrying outsized bergens; America voiced its opinions, and the Dominions. Ambleside's rush-bearing is not so much visited as Grasmere's on the following Saturday, but, like us, this collection of watchers had realized something was afoot and stayed to enjoy it. We all followed the procession to the Market Place, from which for a while the Saturday rush of traffic was diverted. The rush-bearers, all Ambleside, and the visitors, piled into the open space and the result was a mosaic of gay colour. We sang the traditional rush-bearing hymn. At a given signal the bearings were all raised high above the heads of the bearers—a happy sight.

"Our fathers to the House of God,
As yet a building rude,
Bore offerings from the flowery sod,
And fragrant rushes strewed.

May we, their children, ne'er forget
The pious lesson given,
But honour still, together met,
The Lord of Earth and Heaven."

There are four verses, and as the last notes of singing and the last lines of the hymn fade away—

> " He makes to smile the desert place
> With flowers and rushes green ",

the sounds of the town made themselves heard once more and the twentieth century surged back. Then the band struck up and the helter-skelter began again and the procession moved away towards the parish church and the rush-bearing service. There the bearings would be presented and placed proudly in the church, on railings, windows, steps—everywhere where there was room for them. Mr. Ranson's fine mural on the west wall of the church perpetuates such a service. It was painted during the four summer months of 1944 and will keep green a picture of a war-time rush-bearing when the Royal College of Art was in residence in Ambleside. It does not show the one item in the day which is most appreciated by the youngsters—the presentation of ginger-breads; nor hint at the great day when they partake in The Sports.

The old church of St. Anne, where the strewing of rushes was once essential to keep warm the feet of worshippers in winter cold, is in upper Ambleside, on Chapel Hill. Now the small, unpretentious, creeper-clad edifice serves as a church hall. There was a time when Ambleside rejoiced in having this as its own place of worship. Long ago the villagers worshipped either at Grasmere or Bowness church, but finally their little chapel-of-ease was built and in 1675 the chapelry became a parish. Its clergyman was also schoolmaster and not so well paid by modern standards, depending on whittlegate—meals with the families of his scholars in turn, and gifts in kind, to augment his living. Some of the children came from outlying districts, but many doubtless lived in the houses of Old Ambleside—by The Green, Smithy Brow, Tom Fold and Peggy Hill. The most famous of the local schools was that founded by John Kelsick in the reign of George I, to be free to all the boys of Ambleside. Like so many old schools it has much outgrown its founder's expectations. It stands in Grove Road, above the woods which hide Stockghyll. Within the ghyll is the waterfall, Stockghyll Force, and scenery Mrs. Linton a century ago described as "a rough unspoilt bit of rugged beauty happily for the lake world scarcely able to be spoilt even by improvers, so impracticable it is and wild". In Stock valley there was just enough danger and difficulty to delight town-bred tourists "and put fine white feathers in their mountain caps".

Stock Beck played a big part in the village of the past, the waters forming its boundary and turning its mill wheels. One wheel can still be seen from the two bridges, but no longer is it used. The Old Mill is now a studio where the curious stranger can watch some of the old crafts, see modern products of art and craft wedded, and buy souvenirs to carry away with him—paintings, pottery, hand-woven woollens. Above the Old Corn Mill is an ancient Bobbin Mill, a doddering building in the 1840's, when the Horrax family became owners. In the last century it has kept pace with change and modern improvements. When corn mills in Lakeland ceased to be, the saw mill and bobbin mills continued, two of the few existing beckside industries.

Though Ambleside as a town is not itself beautiful, having grown in mid-Victorian days to cater for the increasing flow of tourists, its setting is lovely. "Situs Amabilis", the beautiful place, was its first name, it is said with more sentiment than truth.

> "A Roman host descended from the height
> Of Kirkstone Pass, rock-walled and roofed with cloud:
> Slowly they trod; sudden they cried aloud!
> The mists had risen; what met their raptured sight?
> A golden vale, sun-saturate——"

Coming to the lake head they bestowed upon their camp site—"and surely none will cavil at its fitness or probable truth", writes the Victorian guide—"the name Situs Amabilis".

We cannot tell if the Roman troops at Borrans fort had an eye for beauty, or if to them the lake shore was a frightful uncivilized spot. The fort itself, as plans show, was roughly square, surrounded by a ditch outside enclosing walls in which were gateways—the south gate towards the lake, and in the north-west angle a corner turret. Within the enclosure were four large barracks, a central Principia, or headquarters, a commandant's quarters and a granary. This was the "ancient city with large ruins of walls" described by Camden, who doubted not it was the work of the Romans, "the British bricks, mortar tempered with small pieces of bricks, little urns, glass vials, Roman coins—the round stones like millstones (of which, soldered together, they were wont to make pillars) and the paved ways leading to it, are undeniable evidence". In the eighteenth century West wrote that little seen by Camden remained at "Dictis"—the fort was Galava, according to the latest evidence—"so swift is Time in destroying the last remains of ancient magnificence". From this camp went the Roman ways which we come across when walking through Little Langdale to Wrynose and Hardknott, and, in Eskdale, a road designed by Julius Agricola in the first century A.D. when planning to attack Ireland and put an end to troublesome Irish pirating raids; in Stockdale, above the Troutbeck valley, along High Street and on Moor Divock, and over the fells to Brougham near the Eamont; on the way to Kendal and Watercrook. The excavation before the First World War disclosed many facts about Galava. It had suffered serious attacks with subsequent destruction and rebuilding—at the hands of native Cumbrians.

After the fourth century the camp was left deserted to suffer in turn at the hands of Celt, Picts and Scots, and Scandinavian settlers. Dr. Ekwall believed the name derived from "A melyr satr", meaning a summer shieling by the river sand-bank. Some have thought the name was given by a settler, Hamil, whose "Hamilsett" was among the first of the village communities by the lake.

Ambleside to-day borrows beauty from three lovely dales—Stockdale, Scandale and the Rothay valley. Above Stockdale goes a climbing road which meets the Troutbeck road not far short of the Travellers Rest Inn on Kirkstone Pass. It is a struggle of a road; at lower level are fellside and beckside paths, through birchwoods and hazel copses. Across the valley a green track links the Grove farms, an enchanting path I found one November morning. So few people come higher up the Stock valley than the Force; a great pity.

"About a mile above Ambleside," wrote West, "there is, in a place called The Groves, a cascade that, though the season may be dry, merits a visit on account of its singular beauty and distinguished features—the most curious you will see in the course of the tour." To the scene West gave his highest attributes; Stockghyll Force to him was "highly awful and picturesque". Some years earlier Gray was in Ambleside, but finding the inn impossible—"the best bedchamber dark and damp as a cellar"—he "grew delicate" and passed on to Kendal, thereby depriving us of his early morning impressions of the same fearsome ravine. Keats, however, did stay at Ambleside and in his letters wrote of his early morning, before breakfast, experiences when he "fortunately missed the path and found the falls by the noise of the water". He was so delighted and moved that he declared, "I shall learn poetry here and shall henceforth write more than ever . . . I cannot think with Hazlitt that these scenes make man appear little. I never forgot my stature so completely . . . I live in the eye and my imagination, surpassed, is at rest." After that who can resist the path to Stockghyll?

Above the wooded ghyll the dale is gentler, cradling calm, a place where long ago farmers could drive their stock for shelter when there was rumour of raiders from the north. Climbing Grove Road beyond Kelsick School trees begin to thin, until only rowans, alders and a few wind-bent thorns line the way. The road, too, becomes rough, stony, reaching out to the fells. It crosses merry little becks by ford or primitive bridge, passing Low, Middle and High Grove Farms and entering grass-floored lonnings, ancient walled-in ways, where sheep have gathered in wild weather for centuries, and the grass is nibbled close as a bowling green. At higher level, beyond the farms, the dale assumes wilder aspect, the track defined only by roughly piled walls of boulders, making for the Kirkstone Pass, over acres of rock-ribbed land where winds ripple in the bent grasses and the rush beds, and bring rain-clouds scudding down from the mountains. All around is the peace and loneliness which appeals to the curious traveller of the twentieth century though to earlier comers it was horrid and awesome. The imaginative might hear in the wind the shouts of men in battle over Woundale to the north, the tramping of marching men along the Roman way across Stockdale, the cries of boys herding cattle into hidden depths of the dale when Scots came raiding, and on the wind the voices of those travellers who crossed Kirkstone Pass in the wild days before there was any house or refreshment thereon—cries maybe of those poor souls who lost their way in winter fog or blizzard. Many there were who died.

Stockdale opens out to Ambleside; so does Scandale, which has no through road and is therefore known only to those who seek the charms of the ghyll at Sweden Bridge and then follow the old track to the mountains which connect the Fairfield range with those above Kirkstone. There are great possibilities of quiet here.

The Rothay valley, Rydale, we shall follow on the way north to Keswick. At times the quiet has been banished from this dale, and even from the paths above the river and the lakes, along Loughrigg Terrace and over White Moss, it has been impossible to get out of hearing of road-bound traffic. This cannot, however, rob the Rothay valley of its beauty; at quiet times the enchantment holds us, as it did Dorothy Wordsworth, who recorded the joy she had in it, in her *Grasmere Journals.*

> " Turn where we may, say I, we cannot err
> In this delicious region." [Wordsworth.]

For advice on when to take the Lakeland Tour we can refer to the two early resident guide writers, West and Wordsworth. They disagree at all points.

Father West, who quotes at length from the tours of Thomas Gray and Pennant, says that the first writer " was too late in the season for enjoying the beauties of prospect and rural landscape in a mountainous country: for in October the dews lie long on the grass in the morning, and the clouds descend soon in the evening and conceal the mountains", and Mr. Pennant was equally unfortunate in coming " too early in the spring, when the mountains were mantled with snow, and the dells were darkened with impenetrable mist; hence his gloomy descriptions . . ." As for May, that love-child of the Lakeland months, West said, " Flora displays few of her charms early in May, in a country that has been chilled by seven winter months." For West, winter spanned the months from October to April. " Those, however, who love to see the variety of green and olive tints which appear in the springing and decaying foliage would be much pleased with the sight of the Lakes either in May or September." Given choice, it was from the beginning of June to the end of August for West, for he thought of the landscape most beautifully adorned " in all the trim of summer vegetation . . . robed in every variety of foliage and summer bloom". August enamelled the plain in the richest colours and was best for those who loved " to indulge in botanic studies or who wished to scale the Alpine heights".

Now Wordsworth was quite sure West's " best season" was by no means so: " The colours are of too unvaried a green—and a stronger objection is the rainy weather." How well we know what he meant when he wrote of the rain " setting in with a vigour and continuing with a perseverance". Wordsworth did not completely wipe out holidays at this season for the traveller " in good health or capable of enjoying the forms of Nature in her utmost sublimity". Who would begrudge the confinement of a few wet days or the interruption of his journey " for the sight or sound of a storm coming on or clearing away"? What pleasure there is in "the bold bursts of sunshine, the descending vapours, wandering lights and shadows, and the invigorating torrents and waterfalls, with which broken weather, in a mountainous region, is accompanied". All this lake lovers will vouch for; the most sublime effects are before and after rains.

Wordsworth's preference was for the six weeks following the first of September, and listing the reasons he mentions—harmony of colour, the green aftermath, the standing corn and stubble fields, the colours of the "fern" on the mountain-sides, the changing colours upon the trees. For the best combination of "long days, fine weather, and variety of impressions" late May to late June would best suit the "time-stinted traveller". Dilating on the country joys at this season, Wordsworth is so carried away that there is no need to guess when he would choose to be in Lakeland if he were stinted too.

Those who know the Lakes at all seasons find it most difficult to say which month is best. But for those who are restricted in their time and length of stay I should say—June. And after June—the end of October.

AUTUMN GLORIES AROUND AMBLESIDE

Perhaps those who have never been fortunate enough to see autumn in Lakeland might be interested to read about the Ambleside scene as I saw it in late October and early November, when beauty was poured out with the most lavish hand.

Among the high fells and mountains of Westmorland sunrise comes late. Breakfast was almost over when, looking through an Ambleside window, I saw the smiling morn touching the fell tops with gold and heralding the beginning of another perfect day. Swiftly the light spread along the Fairfield range and into Scandale. Loughrigg remained sombre and unlit, and the roofs of Ambleside were half-hid in morning mist, the parish church completely so, but the cross surmounting the steeple stood out against the sky, touching the top of Loughrigg. For a moment I thought a Calvary had been erected on the fell and that in half an hour I would be standing on the spot.

This morning's wind is playing strange pranks with the church bells; one moment the pealing comes, up-swelling on the wind, the next minute the sound is faint as a memory. High on Loughrigg and out of sight of Ambleside they came near again—windborne.

What a delightful walk it was from Millers Bridge uphill to Brow Head Farm and the golf course! Has any golf course a more beautiful setting? How often must the scenery get in the way of the game! I wonder how long players take to hole the ball on the highest green with so many distractions around them. One couple only were on the course this morning, but I doubt if they paid much attention to the empurpled steeps of Scandale, or to Rydal brilliant under travelling sunlight, or to the north-eastern skyline which spread and increased with every upward stride they took. As I climbed, the Troutbeck fells and the High Street range rose with me. Then the fell gate, the Loughrigg watershed, and beyond another landscape more blue and gold than the first—the Langdale country, Wetherlam, like a blue monster, the varied ups and downs of fell and mountain, and Windermere Lake with Blelham Tarn shining mirror-like in a tawny setting of woodlands.

Meeting people on lonely heights which you have begun to think are yours alone is always something of a shock. I met four people where two paths meet by a peaty pool on the descent to Loughrigg Tarn. They also seemed taken aback. Then we went downhill together, talking of our good fortune, of the weather, of this "the best time of year" in Lakeland, for we agreed, the Indian summer which comes around All Saints' and Martinmas is often more wonderful (and I mean full of reasons for wonder) than the golden days associated with St. Michael and St. Luke.

Time to stand and stare. I had plenty of that, and incentive, too. Writers call Loughrigg Tarn "Diana's Looking Glass", a clear mirror now held up to the beauties of sunlit trees and glowing heights, where last night a passer must have seen the huntress moon within and ripples silvered like fish-scales. Here the wind had dropped, but at Skelwith Bridge smoke blew gustily from the quaint "witch cap" chimneys. Cold winds blew back the foaming water of Skelwith Force. I watched from the woodland path on the Lancashire side of the Brathay. There was a dry whispering accompaniment to my walk through the woods to Colwith Bridge, but only among the oak and beech groves; the pine plantations were dark and silent, and the only movement high above among the tree-tops.

For delicacy of colouring no scene can excel that of the Colwith woods in autumn, for the copses of hazel, birch and rowan stretch from river to fell top—exquisitely lovely. Overtipping the woods I caught sight of High Hackett, "Sarah Yewdale's cottage"—now a ruin—where the little Wordsworths were sent to avoid or recover from the epidemics rampant in Grasmere.

From Colwith to Greenbank and Little Langdale, and here among the swelling green knolls, all was perfect peace—until a roaring stream of threatening language rent the silence. A father, kept waiting for his Sunday dinner, was calling home two of his youngsters. I waited, appalled, for the impending scene of violence. None came. Two little lads came running down a pasture, quite unafraid, passed into a cottage—and peace returned.

LITTLE LANGDALE FARM—VICARS

Beyond the tarn and the last farms of Little Langdale is the Wrynose Pass and the twisting serpent of a mountain road. I shall not go that way to-day.

Reeds are sere and yellow about Little Langdale Tarn, red-rust bracken is reflected in the water. There is not a soul on the road which climbs between the juniper bushes to the ridge hiding Blea Tarn. After such loneliness I expected to find the little hollow about the Tarn deserted. Anyone would think the "Solitary" would live up to its Wordsworthian name now, if ever.

There they would be wrong. Given a good day in October and November, and people throng to the place, all realizing that there within the mountain ring is the best of autumn. There were no less than five people, all drawing the leaning larch when I reached the farm. There is Wordsworth refuted! I do not know if the famous larch was planted when he was a visitor here. Larches in general he condemned as vulgar and alien trees.

> "As a tree it is less than any other pleasing. . . . In spring the larch becomes green long before the native trees and its green is so peculiar and vivid that, finding nothing to harmonize with it . . . a disagreeable speck is produced. In summer . . . it is of a dingy, lifeless hue . . . in autumn of a spiritless unvaried yellow . . . in winter it appears absolutely dead."

Yet some among us approve the decorative quality of the larch in the Lakeland landscape.

From Blea Tarn to Dungeon Gill Hotel I avoided the rough track by a detour over the shoulder of Side Pike. Seen from above, the deep hollow is a compact of all that is tranquil and peaceful. Each time one looks on it this realization comes afresh. And the solid grandeur of the Langdale Pikes in the same way is as staggering each time they appear in the landscape—their immensity and immobility. The sun shone full upon them, picking out the rock buttresses and chimneys where a number of climbers were manœuvring; the ravines held deep shadows. Mickleden, that wide, ice-chiselled dale, is a startling contrast—so smooth and brown, half in sun and half in the long shadows cast by the mountain wall. Soon the sun will dip beyond Pike o' Blisco. It is an hour from sunset, but already the peaks are dividing the light into dazzling shafts.

If you walk in Langdale and have no wish to come in contact with road traffic, you can avoid it. There is the old, the original road, following the beck, bringing one out into the road near Harry Place. You can stop as often as you please for the wonderful backward views without fear of passing cars. And after passing Thrang, where Mr. Luke Walmsley had his studio (people should know his fine stained glass), it is not far to Chapel Stile, where again the road can be avoided. I crossed the wooden bridge over the river and used the slaty path to Elterwater Bridge—revelling in the beauty of foliage and the contrast of golden birches trembling above the dark water. The little wooden châlets of Langdale Estate have a wonderful setting. All was quiet over the river and along the track. Once all was noise and activity when the gunpowder works were in production here, manufacturing seventy years ago over 1,000 tons of explosives every year.

The next mile I will never forget—another to add to many memorable Elterwater experiences. There are some who think little of the attractions of the mere, but they cannot have seen it as I did. As I came along the path from Elterwater village to Skelwith Bridge the sun, dipping behind Tilberthwaite Fells, had charged the clouds with fire. Flame suffused the sky, then the colour ran over the lake, and the trees along the brink were touched with fire. Minute by minute the colours changed, the blinding light became more subdued and mountains, deep purple, took shape against the emblazoned west. As the sky changed from flame to rose, from rose to orange, so the earth colours darkened and deepened until they became black silhouettes; pools of clear green showed among clouds, and channels of primrose yellow. Elterwater held the colour in its still pools. The last I saw of it was bright water rippling under black, dreaming trees and round brackenny knolls.

In haste to Skelwith Bridge, just in time; the last light was going and owls were out a-hunting in the woods I passed through in sunshine this morning. At Clappersgate the lights were winking from windows near and far, and the moon was up behind Wansfell.

AUTUMN BY THE ROTHAY—TO RYDAL AND GRASMERE

One autumn day in October 1801, Dorothy Wordsworth paused, enchanted, to watch one birch tree, a lyric touch in Easedale—" The sun shone upon it, and it glanced in the wind like a flying sun-shiny shower. It was a tree in shape, with stem and branches, but it was like a spirit of water."

What a faithful and accurate observer she was! We feel we know that birch tree as a familiar friend. How she loved birches! It is certainly a queen among Lakeland trees—an Eastern queen in October, though she is " the dainty lady of the woods ", satin-gowned in spring. So often during this October the beauty of the groves of silver birches added magic to scenes already superlatively lovely—at Colwith, at Rydal, in Borrowdale, where I had six of the most perfect walking days, the last of our little Indian summer. But it is one single tree I remember most vividly now, growing from a high rock overhanging the Newton slate quarries on the slope of Loughrigg Fell. The quarries were in afternoon shadow, the workings huge black caves, very silent within and holding still pools, black as Styx. I stood near by, listening to the silence, probing the darkness with my eyes. Then I chanced to look up. Above was the rock and the little birch tree, caught in a shaft of sunlight, a golden tree and every golden leaf trembling and a-shimmer. It seemed to shake itself so that a shower of leaves fell, and many floated downwards to the dark water, dappling it as though with flecks of sunlight.

I turned and looked upon Rydal Water—many birches there, bright and delicate among the heavier foliage of beech and oak, larch and ash, along the shores and on the islets and headlands. The autumn colours, together with the blueness of sky and water and the intense green of the little pastures were such that one seeing them reproduced on canvas would have declared, "Impossible! Exaggerated! Too theatrical!" The colours of late October and early November beggar description in Lakeland. They must be seen to be believed.

Sitting on a boulder on Loughrigg, believing I had the fell to myself, I was suddenly roused by a whistle and barks. On the sky-line a man; racing downhill a sheep-dog giving chase to three sheep. They were brought to a halt on the edge of the beck and soon the farmer was with them, whistling his dog to the gathering-in of two wanderers down by the lake shore. I wondered were they strays from some other farmer's sheep walks, being isolated so that at the Shepherds' Meet they could be returned to their rightful owners. This is the time of year when one meets fell farmers on the passes taking the strays to a fixed exchange point. The Swaledale and cross-bred sheep wander farther afield than the little Herdwicks, which are so firmly attached to their native "heafs" that they rarely roam and are sold with the farms.

The farmer came striding by. "No, they're not strays," said he, "they're a few of my own left out at the last gathering. It's not easy to make a clean gather with all this high bracken. We're giving them the second dipping this week." His were not Herdwicks but cross-breds—"Herdwick yowes crossed wi' a Swardell tup". Herdwicks can weather very hard winters, but when the herbage cannot be reached under ice and snow they refuse a hay diet and succumb, as in 1947.

We had a long sheep talk up on Loughrigg side, in a sunny silence interrupted just once by a great roar from across the lake, a noise which echoed in the ravines.

"Football match," remarked the farmer. "Local side, Grasmere, must have scored a goal agen Sedber."

On to Red Bank and Grasmere; a sun burst, autumn trees afire in it, top branches gilded in the level rays, village fields of an unearthly brilliance. The lake still, a few cruising gulls circling over, and no boat in sight. They lie, upturned, in the boathouses. The church tower is in sun and stained with blood-red creepers; a tree shadow, complete in detail, is thrown upon it.

Grasmere village is itself now. Village life has come into its own and visitors play no part in it. At Wordsworth's grave no pilgrims, but two lads with their backs to it, intent on a cat's movements in search of a mouse. The church interior is dim. I was glad of clear glass in the east window, for it framed a glowing picture, all the autumn glory of mountains sunset-flushed was there. Dove Cottage looked lovely and might have been unutterably sad, as the unlived-in homes of great folk, long dead, always are—in repose—but a robin sang cheerily enough. So small is the cottage, one wonders how the Wordsworths disposed of themselves, a growing family and friends. One October afternoon "thirteen of our neighbours came to tea"—to be entertained by William's bride, the day after her first home-coming.

How Dorothy loved the autumn scene—"the golden woods quiet in their own tranquillity, stately and beautiful in their decaying—the lake a perfect mirror".

Up the old lane to Heugh Fold in enchanted light, for the rays are now pouring between Silver How and Easedale. A little while and it will be twilight. The last person I met was a small girl at White Moss with red ribbons on her pigtails, busy dragging wood to a huge pile for November 5th bonfire. Then a lonely path to Rydal Mount—Wordsworth's path. The sun dips and the mountains are lit from within, like porcelain lamps. The sky is saffron-hued. A wind rises, every tree begins to speak. Leaves shower down, the oak woods are stirred into violent motion. It is a giddy scene. I cannot distinguish between whirling leaves and flying birds.

A farmer tells me the sudden gale is the "ellum wind". The Helm wind coming from Cross Fell and High Cup Nick, sweeping from the east, meeting the mountains and maybe the opposing forces of the west wind, is responsible for "gay queer" goings-on in Lakeland weather. Some friends encountered it yesterday on Striding Edge; possibly it was responsible for a very good turn to me as I passed under the walls of Rydal Mount. A sudden bombardment from above when the gusts caught the Spanish chestnut trees, shaking the branches very thoroughly—and green cases bounced off my head, split on boulders, and shining, sweet chestnuts were there, everywhere, waiting to be gathered in quantities. Light was just enough to allow a "clean gather", as the farmer would put it.

Nearing Ambleside the moon appears, and the lamplighter on his bike. He paused at the old Bridge House, reached up and, hey presto, as pretty a night scene as any.

AMBLESIDE TO GRASMERE—HIGHWAY AND BY-WAYS

Once we are clear of the houses of Ambleside the valley ahead is lovely enough to delight the eyes of any but the most sight-seeing jaded traveller. Sometimes it seems too beautiful for me—too rich, too full to overflowing with colour and perfume; then, the park-like landscape I exchange for the unregulated beauty of the fells above Scandale and Stockdale, or for the heights of Loughrigg or Wansfell. The highway north appealed to tourists two centuries ago, to Gray and the first guide-book writers. It did not run quite on the line of to-day. The road crossed Stock Beck above the watermills—to-day it crosses the Low Stock Bridge—it crossed Rydal Park where Sir Michael Fleming was pleased to allow the appreciative visitor to use carriage drives of his making and to view the landscape from his own summer-house. What would happen now if the appreciative tourist had that privilege extended to him? He would be multiplied a hundred-fold every hour during the tourist season. But not so in the eighteenth century, when a travel-writer could walk in solitary state the "convenient path" and gaze suitably enraptured upon the Rydal Park waterfalls, "seen only through the window of a ruined summer-house in Sir Michael's orchard".

The early traveller did not pass so close to the Bridge House spanning Stock Beck, but many remarked upon it and the artist Turner knew it; he painted the corn mills not far away. In the seventeenth century it was probably a summer-house of the Braithwaites of old Ambleside Hall, though it is not certain whether the little, two-storeyed house was built on an existing bridge or constructed "all of a piece". At one time a thorough-fare must have passed through it. It served as a shop and as the home of a local character who a century and more ago hawked ferns and cried, "Cheers to mend"—old Chairy Rigg.

Nowadays the building and a small plot of ground by the beck are National Trust property and countless more picture-makers can add it to their collection without need to move out of the way of passing traffic; the plot is a tiny oasis of quiet.

Over lower Stock Bridge, on the left of the road, is a house rich in memories and literary associations. Here is The Knoll, the home of Harriet Martineau, who chose the site in the summer of 1845 and had the help and advice of Wordsworth in building it. It became in later years a regular " den of lions " and for the Ambleside natives a source of constant curiosity and conjecture. Miss Martineau was not the sort of woman they were used to. She dabbled in politics, wrote and lectured on highly controversial subjects—and, they whispered, went in the nude to her garden bath-house. Her friends, however, thought well of her and her kindness. The Wordsworths and the Arnolds were frequent guests and received visits from Harriet and her friends. George Eliot visited The Knoll and wrote of Miss Martineau's charm, how handsome she was and intelligent. " She kissed me in the prettiest way this evening, telling me she was so glad she had got me here." Matthew Arnold told a friend of meeting her. " Talked to Miss Martineau—who blasphemes frightfully——" She persuaded him to see her " cow-keeping miracles to-morrow ". A woman of many talents and many interests. Charlotte Brontë thoroughly enjoyed a stay here, for " her house is pleasant both indoors and out, arranged with admirable neatness and comfort. . . . Her visitors enjoy the most perfect liberty . . . I rise at my own hour, breakfast alone . . ." Her hostess, she believed, rose at five, took a cold bath and walked in the starlight of the winter morning.

Though Miss Martineau always left her home at Ambleside " during the Lake season " it was not because she disliked to see large numbers of people enjoying the dales and fells, but " because she wished to avoid the influx of visitors to which she would otherwise be subject ". In fact she was an early defender of the invasion of Lakeland by townsfolk. She could not believe that any inhabitant of the valleys could say with truth " that his happiness had been impaired by the sight of the parties who arrive by steamboat or railway, carrying their provisions and sitting down in the churchyard, or under the trees of some knoll, to have their minds opened and their hearts softened by a spectacle of beauty which gives them for a time a new existence. . . . Let them come, and the more the better, that the more refreshment of spirit may be shed from the fountains of beauty here into the dusty ways of common life in the towns." There spoke a champion of the simple day-tripper.

North of the town the highway crosses Scandale Bridge. What is there here to reveal secrets of its upper dale, rocky ravines with hazels, rowans and hollies, yews and thorns crag-caught and wet with the spray of waterfalls, or of the mountain wastes beyond the upper limit of copse and trees, where the last gate of the Scandale road opens into a vast bowl of bog and bent, crying birds and bleating sheep—a landscape unchanged for a thousand years. The mark of husbandry is not there—save for the sheepfolds by the shallow fords—nor any track save one trodden by shepherds and walkers who take this, one of the most direct routes over to Brothers Water and Patterdale.

Rydal Park lies beyond the beck, green slopes with fine timber well placed upon them, for this landscape is above all planned beauty and the trees the Flemings of long ago planted within their desmesne were placed for landscape beauty as well as for their timber value. Some of the finest oaks and beeches in the dale lie within the Park, and the last survivors of a sisterhood of beeches queen it at the roadside nearing the village—saved in road-widening, the path now running behind them. In summer the Park is the perfect setting for Rydal Sports—not so famous as those of Grasmere, but well supported by a more local crowd of trial and trail enthusiasts. The last time I saw it was a relentless rainy day when hundreds of mackintoshed and sou'westered folk were grouped under trees and among wet boulders, motionless and still, watching with keenest interest the tireless sheep-dogs—hours of trials and dozens of dogs all manœuvring silly sheep in and out of wooden gates and pens. The greatest contrast to all this was the noise and gaudy splashes of colour around the bookies, who shouted their business under brilliant outsize umbrellas. The maximum excitement and movement came with the sighting of the returning trail hounds over the fell top and through the green glades—frantic shouting, whistles and cheers coaxing the animals to that extra bit of effort which marks the winner. And the rain dripped from the trees, slanted across the hills, trickled down the crags, and down how many necks?

Half-way between Scandale and Pelter Bridges on the left of the road is a low knoll with trees upon it, near the point where a footpath runs down to the stepping-stones over the Rothay. Here in the Middle Ages stood the Manor House of the great land-owning Flemings, whose influence in Lakeland dates back to the days of the Conquest, when William rewarded his kinsmen with tracts in Furness and Westmorland. They had halls at Coniston and Rydal; the one by Coniston lake shore was their usual place of residence for generations, Rydal estate coming to them by a marriage in the fifteenth century. In the sixteenth century the manor house on Old Hall Hill was replaced by the more pretentious house below Nab Scar. But it was still standing a century later when a number of Parliamentary soldiers quartered themselves there and, hearing rumour of gold or treasure hidden within the house, began to search under the floors in their usual thorough and destructive manner. Legends later grew up around the ruins; at dead of night the wailing of an infant was heard by timorous countryfolk, who soon spread the story that "T' Aald Hall" was haunted. I have heard nothing more ghostly than the hooting of an owl over the trees, but then I am not attuned to ghosts.

Although this is such a busy highroad the birds seem strangely undisturbed by the traffic. One evening when dusk was gathering over the Rothay at Pelter Bridge I watched a heron brooding over the beck completely oblivious to the noise of a fleet of motor-coaches. Dippers fly purposefully upstream or bob above the swirling currents where the beck washes the retaining wall of the highway as unself-consciously as in the solitude of Easedale Gill or Sweden Bridge. Very few folk saunter along this road; the one on the far side of the Rothay, Under Loughrigg, is better suited to dallying.

On the Hawkshead and Langdale road out of Ambleside, immediately over Rothay Bridge, the Under Loughrigg road turns to follow the river upstream. Between stone walls, unfenced across smooth pastures, against the garden fences of the "most desirable residences", most of them associated with great names of the last century, it goes along the valley floor to Pelter Bridge and Rydal—one of those roads where the stranger has the feeling of straying unawares into a private park. The colour and perfume here, especially on a June day, marigolds at the river's brink, bluebells in the copses at the fell edge, azaleas and rhododendrons blazing in the gardens, everywhere far too much beauty overflowing from this cornucopia. Walking here one May evening in 1800, Dorothy Wordsworth resolved to start a journal and, returning to Dove Cottage, began at once with notes on the charm of this valley. It was a walk she took often to meet the post at Ambleside, to take letters, and to collect letters and papers. She never mentions meeting strangers who were pedestrian tourists on her jaunts to and from Ambleside.

only beggars, "a blind man driving a cow and a beautiful bull", and natives going about their daily business. The friends of the Wordsworths were to be introduced to its pleasures later. One was Dr. Arnold of Rugby School, who brought his family to Fox How—the only house on the right of the road—and during holidays had boys from his school to join them. The Doctor, walking on Loughrigg, declared its beauty excelled that "of Epicurus' garden". His greatest joy was to return here to his "mountain nest" at Fox How, "whose surpassing sweetness I think I may safely say adds a positive happiness to every one of my waking hours passed in it". His son Matthew shared in his feelings.

> "Far from the restless, troubled world withdrawn,
> A poet's dream of river, garden, copse and lawn."

At Loughrigg Holme—a fitting name, for here the gardens are only separated from the Rothay by the road—lived the Quillinans, Edward, a widower, marrying Dora Wordsworth in 1841, and at the house which takes its name from the stepping-stones lived, until the end of the late war, descendants of the poet.

Once only have I seen this green dale looking anything but peaceful. One November morning after torrential rainstorms all the fells were seamed with foaming white water-breaks, all pouring down to meet the already swollen Rothay, with swirling mists still caught on the craggy mountain tops and a great gale sweeping up from Windermere, setting all the riverside trees in violent motion, showering brown leaves upon the floods. And what floods they were!—creeping over the road and filling all the dips in the field beyond, and before the day was over making one long lake of the Vale of Rothay, from Grasmere to Windermere water head.

From Pelter Bridge there is nothing to do but give oneself up to contemplation of the Rydal scene, in any one of many ways. As roads go there are few more blessed with sights—the venerable Lord and Lady Oaks are just behind us—Rydal church, with Rydal Mount, the poet's last home, on the terraced hill-side beyond, where for over thirty years he produced poetry, though it had not quite the authentic "woodnotes wild" of the Dove Cottage days. Here one might have seen Dorothy—but not as we like to remember her, for long years cared for by William and Mary in whose service she had spent herself in the happier, earlier years. Adjoining the garden walls of Rydal Mount is a pretty wooded slope with climbing paths and steps moss-grown or covered with leaves—the Rashfield, which Wordsworth purchased as a possible housing site if ever he were compelled by the Flemings to quit the Mount. When the possibility of a move proved unlikely he gave the land to Dora—hence its name, Dora's Field. No lover of Wordsworth's poetry but will be delighted to linger here awhile—as he is free to do, for the poet's grandson gave it to the National Trust—listening to the birdsong which on spring evenings wins above any sound of traffic, and gazing upon the carpet of woodland flowers—daffodils dancing in April, and bluebells in May.

At one point, where the road hugs the shores of Rydal Mere, is a rock known as Thrang Crag, and to the romantic as the Poet's —that is, Wordsworth's—Seat. Climb the rock steps, sit aloft and after a short session of silent thought you return to the highway " either a poet or a lunatic ". It is rather a damp spot and the mere is screened by a considerable amount of foliage. But we are quite willing to believe that the poet did sit thereon, being a collector of rocks with views, and that poetic thoughts " kindled " him—to use Dorothy's expression for the coming of the divine spark. At one time " lile Hartley Coleridge " lived at the Simpson's farm near by; he must have perched often on the rock like some bright-eyed elf. And De Quincey a-courting the daughter of the Simpsons—did he not gaze with her across the lake on quiet evenings?

Of the scene one can write nothing new. It is and always was pure enchantment:

> " No favoured eye was e'er allowed to gaze
> On lovelier scenes in fairy days."

None—not even the most matter of fact among us can doubt Wordsworth's lines. It is delight to the eyes, in May and June perfume to the nostrils—and always balm and healing to the soul. Tranquillity is there on the smooth bosom of the mere, a mirror held up to the sky, the fells and mountains and the sylvan shores. Every blond reed which has bowed before the gales of winter is a gilt spear in spring thrust into the blue mirror, every stone and boulder against which the wavelets lap and gurgle, every swan, every bird is repeated within the lake. We can lave our hands in the water, linger at the water edge, draw near to all the lovely sandy coves and miniature bays. This is not so by Grasmere Lake.

Mrs. Felicia Hemans, remembering the loveliness of Grasmere, wrote:

"Oh, ne'er may man with touch unhallowed, jar
The perfect music of thy charm serene.
Still, still unchanged, may one sweet region wear
Smiles that subdue the soul to love, and tears, and prayer."

Although man has taken over its shores, the magic still remains. In April 1970 (Wordsworth's centenary month) I was guest speaker at the Cumbrian Literary Society meeting. I had the Prince's room at the Prince of Wales—and pure enchantment from my window.

THE WORDSWORTHS' GRASMERE

Parallel with the highway are two routes by which the walker can link Rydal and Grasmere villages—perhaps the most beautiful short walks in the country. One follows the far shores of Rydal and rises above Grasmere on the lower slopes of Loughrigg—Loughrigg Terrace—and goes on to the upper end of the lake by way of a tree-shadowed road; I have walked it in one and three quarter hours when hurrying to catch a bus back to Ambleside, but I have quite unashamedly revelled in a whole day's loitering here, meeting other loiterers savouring its pleasures in just the same quiet, appreciative way. The second route leaves the highroad by Rydal church, turning along a rough path, over high pastures made lovely by fine, old trees of the Flemings' planting, though some, it is said, are relics of the great mediæval forest of oaks. The path continues without any deviation through copses, through woods full of damp green smells, and on at last to White Moss and the lane which passes the door of Dove Cottage. This is above all a way with memories, every yard was familiar and well loved by all the Wordsworths and their circle of friends. Open Dorothy's journal and many, many references you will find to the small pleasures and discoveries they made walking between village and village.

The highroad was not as we know it when the Wordsworths came to Grasmere; they used the higher and older road from White Moss and over the hill to Heugh Fold, always halting to lean for a moment on the field gate near the highest point, a habit which thousands have since indulged in. If the poems on the

Wishing Gate had never been written it would still have been a spot for leanin', such an exquisite Grasmere landscape is spread out below. This leaning has worn out the upper and lower rungs of several five-barred gates. By the wear and tear alone, no stranger can miss identifying it. A grove of trees across the road was named for John, the beloved naval brother of the Wordsworths. How the breezes play in the topmost branches, green arms waving as in some sylvan ballet. Gray, Pennant, West and all the eighteenth-century tourists journeyed this way through a dale still completely untouched by "modern influences", and looking from the Wishing Gate road saw a sleepy hollow "a little unsuspected paradise" where all was "peace, rusticity and happy poverty in its neatest, most becoming attire". Even the first inn name spelt peace—the Dove and Olive Branch it was called, a low and humble cottage by the wayside destined to be Dove Cottage in later days. Beyond the cottage the old and the Turnpike roads meet to go forward into modern Grasmere, which can hardly live up to Gray's description to-day. The village has grown and changed its character, little rusticity, and certainly no sign of poverty now. As for peace, it comes dropping slow over the lake and over the fells which embrace the hollow, but look for it in vain in the public highway which is the village street. All the world and his wife is at Grasmere on any August day; every city and shire has its name written on the hindquarters of motor-coach and bus parked at the road edge. Beauty always has its disadvantages.

We linger around Dove Cottage; from the door such a stream of folk issues, and all because a brother and sister chose to live there in the years 1799-1807.

The house was bought as a Monument to Plain Living and High Thinking, which was exactly the mode of life enjoyed by the Wordsworths. When Sir Walter Scott came to stay with them he was surprised to see Dorothy and Mary prepare the joint of meat for their dinner in the same room in which it was to be eaten. In so small a dwelling one room had to serve several purposes. What a blessing the garden proved—Wordsworth's study and the children's nursery. Most of the friends they entertained were well content to share in the family life and expected

WISHING GATE

no epicurean feasts which were other than conversational. Scott was rather put out by the lack of interest his host showed in drink stronger than tea; he found himself compelled during his visit to take short walks to the village. On one, Wordsworth tracked him down to the village inn—the Red Lion. Caught glass in hand, Scott was somewhat embarrassed. Perhaps he did not know that Dorothy had been known to bottle rum. Probably she made wines, too, and stalked elderberries or de-petalled cowslips, keeping her hands occupied, whilst Coleridge and her brother talked. Or perhaps she darned or mended William's shirts or "made a shoe"—or baked bread and pies—or broiled her guest a mutton chop. It would have been good to eavesdrop at one of the open casements when the friends were talking within—of their literary hopes and aspirations, of Coleridge's plans, of the day's experiences which often found their place in Dorothy's journals and inspired William to poetry.

Times have changed indeed since the day when Dorothy Wordsworth, sitting on the wall of the little front garden, was very gratified to see the occupants of a coroneted landau turn round for a second glance at the simple cottage. Thousands now give it much more than a glance. They come from every corner of the earth, bespectacled students from U.S.A., Asiatics, earnest Wordsworthians from Scandinavia, and queues of Britons for whom in many cases this visit is just one of the "done things" when visiting Grasmere and just a curious "in-and-out-the rooms" of what they consider a very dark and cramped cottage. Some hear voices from the past—"I wandered lonely as a cloud" recited in childish monotone; some remember childhood copy books—"Wordsworth wrote 'The Pet Lamb', 'Lucy Gray' and 'We Are Seven'." But a visit is a richer experience for those who come with well-prepared minds. These are not empty rooms, forlorn, melancholy, but peopled with memories. Wordsworth is there, his fine head silhouetted against the window, Dorothy, head lowered, is writing to his dictation, Mary is in the background with the little children about her knees. Steps on the path; maybe it is a passing pedlar, one of the neighbours, maybe Coleridge come over from Keswick, maybe Southey; the rumble of carriage wheels heralds the coming of the Bard of the North, or Mrs. Coleridge with her children on their way from the south to Keswick, with young Mr. De Quincey as their escort, a very shy young man who had longed for a meeting with the poet but had never had the courage to do more than look at Dove Cottage from afar.

De Quincey also becomes part of the Dove Cottage interior. He took over from the Wordsworths in 1809 and lived there for twenty years, surrounded by his library of books, taking comfort from his opium and his dreams. "This was the scene of my struggles, the most tempestuous and bitter in my own mind, this the scene of my despondency and unhappiness, this the scene of my happiness," he wrote in his *Confessions*. He was not entirely alone. Like the Wordsworths he had a constant flow of visitors at his door—the Wordsworths themselves and their friends, who were De Quincey's also, and later to share his hearth came the daughter of the Simpsons of Nab Cottage, Margaret—" her arms like Aurora's and her smile like Hebe's"—to be his wife and helpmate.

From Dove Cottage the road goes into "new" Grasmere, through the village to the Rothay Bridge and the church. Here we linger awhile, leaning over the parapet to watch the trout darting through shadowed pools. Like everyone else who comes to Grasmere church we follow arrow-marks to the Poet's Grave, a railed-in plot wherein lie the Wordsworths and their nearest friends. What might have been the quietest corner of the graveyard is the most visited. People come—some with ice-cream and their lollipops; some know why they come, some are rather hazy about the whole "pilgrimage". They pass on near the yews, newly planted in Wordsworth's days and protected from harm by railings bought by him, through the lychgate to the gingerbread shop. If they are lucky they buy gingerbread—if there has been baking on the day of their visit; there is a secret, guarded recipe, and no eyes look on whilst it is made, whilst the rest of Grasmere sleeps.

We return to the church. It is as the poet knew it, the roof

"upheld
By naked rafter, intricately crossed,
Like leafless underboughs, 'mid some thick grove,
All withered by the depth of shade above—
Admonitory texts inscribed the walls—
Each in its ornamental scroll enclosed——"

This is the church of The Excursion, though many of the naked rafters in the nave roof have crumbled before the onslaught of that terrible scourge, the death-watch beetle, and new sound timber has replaced them. In the chancel the monuments and memorials of the Flemings are in place and the texts painted on dark boards; massive coats of arms, relics of the eighteenth century, overtop the east window.

I wonder if the Wordsworths knew Jemima Bridges, whose epitaph is one of the gems of the church. Her death in 1822 was mourned thus:

> "These vales were saddened with no common gloom
> When good Jemima perished in her bloom;
> When, such the awful will of heaven, she died
> By flames breathed on her from her own fireside."

LYCHGATE—GRASMERE

That was tragedy indeed, and so was the death of John and Sarah Green, who perished in a terrible snowstorm on the mountain path between Langdale and Easedale Tarn whilst their family of small children waited for their return in the little house down in the valley. Their grave is by the path to the lychgate.

Essential quiet broods within the church. For a little while we merge with the tourists again, then on into the little lane leading to Butterlyp How, Goody Bridge and Easedale, where peace lies dreaming over the beckside pastures and all the way to the down-dropping cascades, Sour Milk Falls. Climbing the stony path to the left of the falls, we make our way across the wasteland of boulders, bracken and bog-grass to the intermont valley wherein great mountains cradle the lonely tarn, and we know why Lakeland calls so strongly to lovers of wild and lonely places. Come here in high summer when a drowsy haze lies over the waters and there is not a movement in the cloud-laid shadows placed on the mountain-sides; come in autumn when no mist can quite quench the burning, flaming glory; or come on a lively morning in early spring, blown along by a boisterous wind which showers spray from the falls and plays arpeggios across the tarn —from the boathouse to the farthest crag.

This is no highway, only a route trodden for a thousand years by neighbour farmers and shepherds whose sheep walks lie on Langdale Pikes and Serjeant Man, a short-cut between Langdale and the Vale of Grasmere.

There is no need to stray quite so far to escape from the throng. But a few minutes from the church along the same lane there is a high knoll which Dorothy Wordsworth soon discovered when she first came to Grasmere, a place to climb and sit in the sun, overlooking the dale, the lake and the mountains. Butterlyp How is the nearest Grasmere possesses to a Castle How or Castle Rock—every dale has one in its throat—but nothing of its history is known. It is a wonderful viewpoint and as it is National Trust property there is nothing to prevent one dallying on its crown as long as the mood lasts. The sound of traffic comes from the highway as it begins its formidable climb to the pass, Dunmail Raise—but it can be forgotten. The birds put up a good concert performance; The How is encircled by flowering bushes and trees, feathered choristers "go it" from dawn to dusk, the full-throated throstle cutting out the sounds of throbbing engines.

Turning westwards from Butterlyp How we overlook a well-wooded parkland, surrounding the house called Allan Bank, wherein the Wordsworths lived for three rather uncomfortable years. Three adults and three small children had begun to feel the extreme smallness of Dove Cottage irksome; they were indeed "crammed in their little nest edge-full". A Mr. and Mrs. Crump had built for themselves, in a most desirable spot north of the lake, a house which the Wordsworths considered a "temple of abomination", for it stared them in the face from every part of the dale; they declared it was out of keeping entirely with the rest of the simple architecture of Grasmere. Actually the house was a herald of hundreds of other "desirable residences" which were in the next few decades to spring up in all the loveliest parts of Lakeland. As Dorothy wrote, since the house was there they might as well live inside it as be compelled to look at it from without; when it was offered to let by the Crumps they at once rented it and moved "lock, stock and barrel" from the cottage. Not much of their old furniture was suitable so—like many other householders with modest incomes—they began to frequent local sales, wandering as far afield as Coniston and returning laden with sale bargains. Sales never lost their appeal; they were still hunting bargains when they went to live at Rydal Mount.

Whatever they said of the raw ugliness of the new house externally, the views from the windows left nothing to be desired—they were "delicious" and the great mountains, Fairfield and Seat Sandal—which filled the front windows—and the village nestling at their feet, the "bonny cottages with their tufts of trees" and the pastures in the valley floor made a "soothing scene". Dorothy did have regrets at times for the cottage, but she appreciated the roominess of Allan Bank and the "comfort of having each a room of our own".

The soothing scene from the windows was about the only feature which proved soothing in the new home. If Dorothy wanted a little peace she found it revisiting Dove Cottage garden on the days when she went to the old home, helping De Quincey to settle in. Dove Cottage had been a busy house, but at Allan Bank——! At the outset sister-in-law Sarah Hutchinson, who was living with them, became ill. William was to do nothing. Mary sprained her arm and was *hors de combat.* The sailor brother of the Hutchinsons proved a friend in need, a handy man about the house who helped Dorothy to get things shipshape. Five adults and three children—with De Quincey staying with them for some months, Samuel Taylor Coleridge a long-term resident, his two sons, who attended school in Ambleside, coming to Allan Bank for the week-ends—and two more babies arriving at intervals; such was the personnel. The house itself proved very hard to run; it had been badly planned and built, the fires smoked perpetually and Wordsworth's eyes suffered much from this time onwards—they all had smarting eyes—the cellars were damp, there were long draughty passages and doors constantly slamming in the wind, the half-furnished and half-carpeted rooms looked bare and barrack-like, there was endless cleaning and perpetual noise, the children had whooping cough and had to be sent off to Sarah Yewdale's farm at Hackett, overlooking Colwith. When the three years' tenancy was ended none was really sorry to leave to take up residence in the Rectory at Grasmere—where the old-fashioned furniture looked much happier than in its

Allan Bank setting, and where they could start attending church regularly, "so good for the children".

Allan Bank to-day is no longer a raw and ugly house, for time and nature have combined to soften its bleak outlines. Would visitors to-day cry aloud against "this desecration of the Grasmere scene"? When I visited the house in 1947 it seemed to me a most pleasant dwelling, both gracious and pleasing, and certainly not a bare and comfortless place. The rooms are named after the Wordsworths and their friends who visited them here; the room to the left of the hall door, which was Wordsworth's Study—or would Library be the better name?—has views from the wide windows quite as lovely as those which soothed the harassed Dorothy over a hundred and seventy years ago. The trees stand proudly in the Park hiding some of the view seen when the house was new, but the raking steeps of the high mountains still bound the east; lovely gardens such as the Wordsworths never knew surround the house. Here lived Canon Rawnsley, who gathered together so many memories from old people who had known the Lake poets and who began a work which would have been dear to the heart of the brotherhood of poets had they been alive a century later. Canon Rawnsley and Octavia Hill are the two names which will never be forgotten as founders of the National Trust; its beginnings were in Lakeland, but how far its influence has spread! The Canon's widow was a great Wordsworthian. My visits to Allan Bank were memorable. She gave me plants,—descendants of campanulas planted by the Wordsworths, and cuttings from shrubs given her by Reginald Farrar. Above all I value what she wrote of my Lakeland books. Praise from her was praise indeed.

It was mentioned to Mrs. Rawnsley that I had written a book on Lakeland—*Off To The Lakes,* which was published after my visit in 1948. "I wish it every success," she said. "You join a noble army of writers," and led me into the room where Wordsworth wrote so much of his poetry. It was shelved from floor to ceiling, each shelf lined with books, some old, some new, some slim, some mighty volumes. "Each one is about the Lakes or by some Lakeland writer," I was told. There must have been hundreds, even thousands of books. I felt very humble—and, for a whole day, very sad. I handled some of the books—some were early editions of Wordsworth's works which arrived by post unbound and were at once bound by some female members of the family in scraps left over from their dressmaking. There was a first edition of *The Excursion*—written in this room, and signed by other great poets who had been friends of the Rawnsleys—Robert Bridges, Austin and Masefield.

From Butterlyp How we retrace our steps to the village, the shops and the inns. The Red Lion was the most frequented of the old inns a century and more ago, a lively village social centre as well as halting-place for tourists. A hundred years ago, when the rush-bearing had its utilitarian as well as its entertainment value, the rush-bearers retired to the inn after the ceremony was over. They had had a long day and doubtless felt in need of refreshment and conviviality. Early in the morning the young women of Grasmere, with one who was chosen queen among them, went to gather green rushes. The queen plaited and twisted her burden into an ornate shape, the rest piling theirs into large sheets which were carried in procession into the churchyard. A service was held, the rush-bearing hymn sung and the cold, stone-flagged floor strewn with rushes deep enough to provide a covering for the autumn and winter months. The queen's burden was deposited for a few days in the chancel. A simple ceremony with a definite purpose; Grasmere and Ambleside still uphold the old tradition, but in these days of church heating rush-strewn floors are no longer needed. Most of the young people in recent rush-bearing processions weave their burdens into shapes more ornate and fantastic than any to which the former queens aspired. There is still "rustic revelry", but not as in 1827, when a writer described how the villagers adjourned to the ballroom in the hayloft of the Red Lion (then the inn of Mr. Bell) "to trip it merrily and heavily—I called it thumping", to the fiddling of Billy Dawson. They kept up the dancing till almost midnight, when the rector, anxious that the merriment should end before the Sabbath, sent across his servant with a most tactfully worded message: "Master's compliments and will thank you to lend him your fiddling stick?" Whereupon the dancing ended and the lads and lasses trooped homeward to the scattered cottages and farms.

Mr. Fleming, the rector in 1827, was not like the Grasmere cleric of whom Wordsworth wrote in his preface to *The Epistle*, a Mr. Rowlandson, a curate who had a liking for strong drink but was never seen intoxicated "at his own expense". One summer morning the poet found him sitting on the turf by the roadside somewhere near Red Bank; the curate had been carousing over in Langdale and was not quite recovered from the effects. It was a scene of perfect beauty which stretched before him. He was touched by it and heard to say, "Good God, that

I should have led so long such a life in such a place!" The poet later remarked dryly that he did not notice much marked improvement. Avarice was one of Rowlandson's faults and carried to such an extent that in his retiring years he would not pay hired labourers to tend his fields for him and was seen "in his half-dotage working his hay in the month of November by moonlight"; certainly a melancholy sight.

Grasmere to so many visitors is merely a very good centre for a valley chock-full of beauty spots. They forget it has a village life and played a part in the social history of England just as much as Chipping Camden or Bideford. I like to read of doings of a century and more ago, of rush-bearings, of fair days—"Very few people and very few stalls, yet I believe there were many cakes and much beer sold . . . the moonlight shone only upon the village . . . sounds of merriment and dancing came on the still air", wrote Dorothy Wordsworth one fair day.

OVER THE RAISE TO THIRLMERE AND KESWICK

Modern travellers who turn not a hair on the most fearsome Alpine passes and mountain roads of Norway, who have crossed Grossglochner unperturbed, must find incredible Defoe's horror on entering the Westmorland mountains and approaching Dunmail Raise:

> "In a country all mountainous and full of innumerable high hills it was not easy for a traveller to judge which was highest. Nor were these hills high and formidable only, but they had a kind of inhospitable terror in them. Here were no rich, pleasant valleys between them—and this part of the country yields little or nothing at all . . . Westmorland, a county eminent only for being the wildest, most barren and frightful of any that I have passed over—the west side which borders on Cumberland is indeed bounded by a chain of almost unpassable mountains . . . But it is of no advantage to represent horror as the character of the country in the middle of all the frightful appearances to right and left——"

Defoe was not prone to let natural scenery get the better of him. This was actually Westmorland unseen, or only seen afar, from the Kendal-Appleby road. Had he travelled Dunmail Raise what would his emotions have been?

I do not know who was the first to see the lamb and the lion in the rocky crown of Helm Crag—some see the rocks as a lady at an organ—but in the eighteenth century the crag was "an immense mass of antediluvian ruins", or, to Thomas Gray, "like some gigantic building demolished and stones that composed it flung across each other in wild confusion". Everyone knows the crag; everyone also connects the pass with the British King Dunmail, though few know why. Some are told that a pile of stones at the summit of the pass is the burial place of the last British king of Cumbria—the land of the Cymri, and that his royal crown lies deep within the dark tarn of Grisedale—high in the clouds of Helvellyn. It is true that somewhere in this region a battle did take place in which Dunmail or Donal was defeated by Edmund, the Anglian king, but Dunmail lived on in some monastery and Edmund handed Cumbria to the King of Strathclyde, an unfortunate move which for centuries gave the Scots the feeling that this corner of England was theirs to have and to hold; hence the continuous Scots raids.

The road is a long drag; the wandering lane which creeps along the feet of Helm Crag, linking Thorney How, the Youth Hostel, and Under Helm Farm and the farmyard at Town Head, cuts off part of the highway when we are not compelled to travel surfaced roads. Charming it is, between crumbling old walls—tiny yellow poppies and violets grow against them in May—and very near to the craggy fell.

As a viewpoint the Raise is superb. It halted the early tourists whether in chaise or on horseback; they stood and gazed enraptured on all "the possible variety of cascades, waterfalls and cataracts bounding from rock to rock in foaming torrents, hurling huge fragments to the vale that make the mountains tremble in their fall". That was after a wet season, surely. To the east they gazed upon "a chaos of nameless mountains and crags on whose precipitous fronts the eagle builds his nest secure from the envious shepherds of the vale". They were not blessed with detailed maps in those days and were blissfully ignorant of all but a few of the mountain names. They had to accept those local countryfolk gave to them and write them down phonetically. Beyond the Raise they descended into a bare and lonely hollow. "Silver streams poured into it from the mountain sides and warbling joined the dale," wrote one. Now the streams still flow, some in regulated channels; now the little lake, Lees or Leathes Water, or Wyburn or Wythburn Water, is a great sheet called Thirlmere and Manchester reaps the benefit of the stored element. Old drawings show a shepherds' bridge spanning the lake where two arms almost cut it in half; barren slopes reached down to the water's edge, a favourite loitering spot with all the Wordsworths when bound to and from Keswick, and a frequent place of meeting with Coleridge. Brother John was fond of fishing in Wythburn Water, catching pike. At the first hamlet, by the lake, at Wythburn, was the little chapel of ease to St. Kentigern's of Crosthwaite, a typical house of prayer for the community of mountain folk. Of Wythburn chapel it was written by Hartley Coleridge:

> "Humble it is and very meek and low,
> And speaks its purpose with a single bell,
> But God Himself and He alone can know
> If spiry temples please Him half so well."

Its clergyman, called a Reader, received the princely sum of £2 10s. yearly for his services, but eked out his meagre living by the "extras"—one new suit a year, one pair of clogs, two pairs of shoes, a shirt and knitted stockings, and he received whittlegate—two or three weeks feeding at the tables of each of his parishioners—and certain pasture rights for his own beasts, and goosegait, on the common, on Helvellyn's breast.

What type of man this Reader was we know from a fund of old tales; none were men of learning and what discourses came from the pulpit were not above the heads of the hearers. One clergyman lost his stock of sermons—he had two—but his loss in no way perturbed him. He opened his Bible; "My sermons have got down t' grike in't pulpit," said he, "but I'll read you something out of Job worth both of them put together." Many such tales are recorded of Cumbrian parsons of the eighteenth century—men who were not averse to bringing a service to a speedy end because of the chance of a bit of sport, a fox hunt maybe, or thought nothing amiss in discussing business matters—the case of a stray sheep or sale of a heifer, over the edge of the pulpit. The churchyard at Wythburn, a place of meeting, must have heard a variety of topics on Sunday mornings. Usually the talk was continued in the hospitable inn next door, where the churchgoers left their nags—and gave the inn, the Nag's Head, its name. Some sought refreshment before the service; Sir Richard Fleming of Rydal Hall, who worshipped at Wythburn, was often "stiddied up the aisle" after a bout of good cheer with his cronies. Sevenpence was the price of a breakfast fit for a king at the Nag's Head—slices of mutton ham, fried eggs, tea, were served to hungry climbers who came down from Helvellyn early in the morning. Its rival, the Cherry Tree, also had its patrons, among them Wordsworth's waggoner, who heard the sound of fiddling and jollity as he came near: Wythburn was enjoying its Merry-night—

"Blithe souls and lightsome hearts have we,
Feasting at the Cherry Tree."

Ale was flowing, music playing, feet stamping, and at the end of each jig (according to Wordsworth's footnote) the Rustic had the agreeable duty of kissing his partner.

Changes have come to Wythburn; there are no dalesfolk here now to take part in rustic revelries. The farms from which they came are drowned beneath the waters of the new lake, the valley is "sterilized"; the little old church demands a passing glance from the tourist—it was "one of the smallest churches" and tourists love extremes—the Cherry Tree and the Nag's Head are no longer licensed and one must go to the northern end of Thirlmere, to Thirlspot, to find the open door of the King's Head. Everyone knows the King's Head—it is a bus stop, a coach halt, and has a long history as a travellers' rest. It was usually called John Stanley's in the early nineteenth century, John being a character among innkeepers, a Boniface of the old school. The Nag's Head claimed to have a sign painted by the great artist Romney—who was born at Dalton and died in Kendal—but the King's Head boasted an effort of John's, a poetic sign.

"I, Stanley, lives here and sells good ale;
Come in and drink it before it goes stale.
John succeedeth his father, Peter,
But in t'ould man's time it was never better."

Dorothy Wordsworth tells of a visit here in Christmas week 1807 when she came over the Raise with William and his wife: "We carried some cold mutton in our pockets and dined at John Stanley's, where they were making Christmas pies . . . there we roasted apples in the room." There are still some wayside inns where walkers can look for the same kind of easy homely conditions.

The highroad to-day from Wythburn to Thirlspot plays hide and seek with the new lake, passing through plantations of conifers here. and with views across the dark lake there, the scene pleasing enough to travellers who know nothing of the natural unspoilt beauty of more fortunate lakes, but touched with sadness to those who prefer lakes to reservoirs. Eighteenth-century tourists would not recognize the dale now. I picked up for sixpence each some old engravings of Lakeland scenes, in a tray outside a bookshop one day; one showed this valley with the small lake, or rather two lakes, with a wooden bridge spanning the narrow neck between them and bare, treeless slopes reaching down to the water's edge. This was then the landscape which charmed so many old travel-writers and seekers after the history of old Cumberland. It had its hall at Armboth—with tales of hauntings and spectres, there was a ghostly hound which swam across the water, at Launchy Gill was the meeting-place for the tenantry of the dale, a "moot" for law making, on the fell above was the stone where local spinners and weavers met in the plague years to hand over their work to the cloth merchants, in the dale bottom were wandering paths and more direct "chapel stiles" leading to the church and the inns. It was so fair a valley that Wordsworth in his Guide advised travellers afoot to enquire at Wythburn for the way to the west side of the lake and there to proceed at leisure to the foot where "the Wyerburn stream" emptied the lake and entered the Vale of St. John's. Most of us prefer to walk the west side of Thirlmere, looking across to the steeps of Helvellyn; better still, we climb up the fellside from Dob Gill, rise above the tree-line and see Helvellyn in all its majesty. The road-user never sees the giant from Thirlmere shores.

When I called for a meal at the King's Head I was glad to find a dish of rum butter was on the table; a welcome return in post-war austerity. Some other guests, not knowing the confection—and who was to blame them, for it is a typical Cumberland product—thought it was a salad dressing. They soon found their mistake. Rum cannot be disguised, and since the days when, they say, eighteenth-century smugglers carried kegs of rum over the passes to the dales farmers, farmwives have known what to do with it. They made rum butter by melting farm butter and soft brown sugar in a pan, adding nutmeg and spices, then adding rum; the best cooks put in a quarter bottle of rum to a pound and a half of butter and three pounds of sugar. And it was served at births, christenings, Christmas and on all occasions of thanksgiving.

I was interested to learn just how much of John Stanley's old hostelry was preserved in the modern inn. In various rooms were seventeenth-century cupboards and tables and over the bar a piece of carving of Jacobean date, but no sign of Stanley's "good ale" invitation. The present landlord was busy dispensing refreshment to a number of local men in the bar—all home returning from Hound Trails at Ambleside and two with hounds lying docile at their feet—but he spared a few minutes to tell me what he knew. Of the inn sign he knew nothing, but one man put down his glass to recall lines of a carving he had once known, obviously a later inn sign. "There were six lines of pottery—summat about no sensible mare will pass this inn. Later on it got taken into stables and used to fill up sides of a stall—then someone must have taken a fancy to it. It disappeared." The landlord, Mr. Gaskell, showed where the old part—the bar, passage and "till yon steps go down"—had been enlarged. This half, with the large adjoining stable—now used for cars—must have been there a century ago. The stabling was ample for the horses used to speed the post-coaches on their way to and from Keswick. When the coach horn sounded the innkeeper, who was also postmaster, used to empty the posting box which still fills a small window in the bar—it has a perpendicular slot for letters—and he handed them to the driver of the mail coach. Southbound, the coach then crossed the beck which used to flow, unwalled, unprotected, in front of the inn—cows from the adjoining shippons ambled over a low pack-horse bridge into open pastures—and the old highway ran along the dale floor, where the lake now lies, and climbed again to the Wythburn inns.

Beyond Thirlspot; no more dark pine and spruce plantations, only green ridges where oaks grow, not "as they are told", and the eye can sweep the western flanks of Helvellyn to the sky-line. One poet scanning those steeps found a rhyme for the mountain name. There, said he, high above us was the grave of Sir Arthur O'Kellyn.

"His sword is rust,
His bones are dust,
His soul is with the saints, I trust."

A short distance onwards a waterfall leaps down the rocks on the right of the road, Fisher Ghyll its name, and the pretty buff-walled house below, which has a white-walled and lowlier neighbour with dark clipped trees in its garden, is Fisher Place, the home of Hall Caine, who brought here his friend, Dante Gabriel

Rossetti. At the time the great pre-Raphaelite was sick, indeed a dying man, but seeing this very lovely spot for the first time and casting his eyes over dale and fell he declared, "I'm not one of those who care much about scenery, but this is marvellous. . . . The scenery is the most romantic and beautiful that can be conceived and the retirement more absolute than I ever met before."

There is still delight to the eye and solace to the soul hereabouts—at the quiet times of day, on the June evening, for instance, when I wandered on slowly from the inn to Legburthwaite and along the river banks through the Vale of St. John's. I left the highway to the stream of motor-coaches and buses. I think mine the better choice for anyone who prefers the footpath approach to Keswick. In the 1960's A591, my "Most Beautiful Road", was improved out of all recognition, upgraded to become a major trunk road robbed of its character. Who would now recognise Thomas Gray's "good country road, through narrow and stony but sound lanes, very safe in broad daylight" in today's dual carriageways? It is more likely to drive walkers off now than when I escaped from it twenty years ago!

Two dalesmen were sitting on the wall at the road end by Legburthwaite. They asked if I had news of the Hound Trail winners at Ambleside. I had not, though earlier in the day I had heard all the clamour of baying hounds borne across the Rothay valley from Ambleside Park. From talk of hounds we passed to the topic of weather, the lateness of the spring, the snow still lying high on east-facing Helvellyn gullies—where Keswick youths had found good ski-ing well into May. This year many Cumbrian heights carried into June December snows, but for the most part the snow was that left from Easter blizzards which caused so many tragedies on Lakeland mountains. The two men told of the discovery of a bus driver some days after Easter 1951, who saw not far from the highway above Thirlmere the body of the Todmorden walker who had been lost whilst crossing from Patterdale; when exhaustion and cold overcame him he was within shouting distance of this busy road. Only when the lower slopes were cleared of snow was the body discovered. Just over the sky-line where Deepdale eats its way from Patterdale to Fairfield two girl walkers were lost during the same tragic week-end. "And," said one of the men, "there might well have been four others too. I stopped four who were gannin' off ower t'tops till Patterd'le. I warned 'em what they were in for wi' snow whirling round. They were for clammering ower t'mountain in spite of what I said. A bit thick they were. Anyhow, I got 'em turned back to St. John's and told 'em to make for Matterdale End."

Near where we talked was the tiny church of Legburthwaite, served together with that of Wythburn and St. John's in the Vale. This is not an old building as are the other two, but it has a commendable simplicity and within peace comes dropping very slowly. On the door is an invitation to enter. This little house of prayer, "Lying under the range of mighty Helvellyn, speaking of stability and eternity, is a witness of God's unchanging and eternal love in this world of everchanging values". The Communion table is rough-hewn timber with the bark still upon it. All the furnishings are in keeping with the simplicity of the little church and with the community of foresters it serves. The woodmen work in the Thirlmere plantations of the Manchester Waterworks, some care for the nursery of seedlings and young trees by St. John's Beck, some are woodcutters in the conifer groves, others work in the saw mills near Legburthwaite where the pine and fir thinnings are sawn into pit props and impregnated with creosote in special tanks. A week or two before Christmas lorries go away to Manchester laden with spruce-tree toppings—for Christmas trees. Mr. John Edwards, who was in charge of the Manchester afforestation, once worked in the royal forestry at Balmoral, often with the interested eye of King George V upon him. The King was keenly interested in tree planting.

A great crag, cried over by countless homing rooks, overshadows the dale here. Castle Rock gilded by the evening sunlight is an enchanting sight, a vision out of an old romance. With little imagination one can create towers and battlements from rock, trace staircases up the giddy steeps and out of the charmed air detect strains of music more than earthly. Sir Walter Scott saw Castle Rock and envisaged the magic Castle of Triermain, weaving about it the tale of the sorceress who was the undoing of King Arthur—not the blameless knight of Tennysonian Idylls, alas—and of the nymph who was to cause the destruction of his Table Round. The poet was staying at the Royal Oak at Keswick when writing his *Bridal of Triermain* and found St. John's an inspiring dale. The road from Thirlmere to Threlkeld and Penrith passes at the foot of the rock. Across the river a bewitching path goes down dale to Low Bridge Farm and a grass-grown track, an ancient way to the old church goes up and down, up and down, through the loveliest secluded nooks of the fells. Every mile is charming, and not only in June. I was blessed. For me the sun cast brilliant light on the farther slopes of the dale, brightening the apricot-coloured flanks where last autumn's bracken had not yet been covered with the pale green of new shoots, turning the larches into an unearthly green, picking out rowan trees and thorns white with blossom at high level, banks of golden gorse and drifts of bluebells at the foot of the fells. The dale floor is here divided into fields of brilliant emerald—some seamed with runnels full of marsh marigolds, some pale mauve with cuckoo flowers; over

CASTLE ROCK—ST. JOHN'S VALE

all a cuckoo called without discrimination. When I rest on a boulder a young hare dashes almost across my feet; his alarm when he discovers me is comical. He jumps widdershins about and like lightning is away again. On the sky-line a figure appears and a shepherd whistles to his dog. Sounds re-echo against Wanthwaite Crags. Every cuckoo has two voices in this dale.

As I sat surveying this charming valley I recalled an account given in West's Guide of a devastating storm in August 1749 when a cloud-burst swelled all the streams, deluged the whole valley, and " several thousands of huge fragments of broken rocks were driven by the impetuosity of these dreadful cataracts into the fields below . . . some of them more than ten horses could move and one nineteen yards in circumference". A miller, infirm and in bed, rose after the storm to behold "nothing but ruin and desolation . . . his mill and the stable having been swept away, leaving the dwelling-houses standing in the middle, rent open at both ends". He saw the vale covered with stones and rubbish four feet deep, among which one of his precious millstones was lost. Devastation stretched to Legburthwaite and Fornside "but happily through the providence of the Almighty no person's life was lost".

The track climbs high and at its highest point Blencathra fills the sky to the north, its lovely curves hyacinthine blue. Skiddaw, its loftier sister, does not dominate the scene until I am leaving the church of St. John.

How beautifully sited the church is, on a high ridge between the two dales—Naddle and St. John's own. A simple slate-built church with a tiny bell turret, it was rebuilt in 1846, but against the west end of the churchyard is a well basin—icy water within it—and a seat for the wanderer. They call it St. John's Well, but what antiquity is imputed I do not know. There are places in Wales and Cornwall and Western Scotland where clear "kelds" such as this were known to have been used by hermits, holy men, saints, who built near at hand their humble cells. There they ministered to the needs of the countryfolk in the early days of the church. There in later years small churches were built. I would like to think the priests who followed St. Kentigern to Crosthwaite came here to convert the mountain folk to Christianity. I drank the water from the chained leaden cup and thought of what might have been. Inside the church the east window shows Christ as the Good Shepherd. Outside the walls the world is full of the bleating of ewes and lambs, of curlews crying, of the full-throated song of blackbird and thrush, and the lesser, joyful notes of robin and chaffinch. I might well be many miles from the busy highway, yet less than a mile away after descending to the lush green pastures by Naddle Beck—fishes here leaping from the deep pools—I hit the hard road near the farms called Nest. Keswick was but a short distance to the north.

KESWICK AND THE NEIGHBOURING DALES

When the rains pour in relentless torrents down the mountains and there is no visible sign of the clouds breaking, Keswick is most desirable to me; when the sun shines I am always anxious to put the little town behind with all speed. It is good to waken up on a smiling morning in Keswick to see the mists lifting from the Catbells and the Borrowdale mountains, "a great camp of single mountains each in shape resembling a giant's tent", taking form out of the clouds; it is good to look down upon the town late in the evening when an arc of lights twinkles from the blueness of the lake edge and the "giants' camp" is drawing back into the pall of night. Keswick is an old town, the "cheese-wick" or dairy farm of Norse settlers; it was given its market charter by Edward I, it became a centre of trade for the shepherds of the fells, the farmers of the Derwent valley, for the miners who worked at different periods the gold and copper of Newlands, the wad of Borrowdale, and for the quarrymen who lived about the feet of Skiddaw. The Cumbrian Celts from their mountain fastnesses were taught of Christ by Scotland's beloved St. Mungo—St. Kentigern his real name—and his cross was erected in a clearing by the place where "the river of the oak trees" emptied from the one lake to flow over the swampy flats into the lower lake of "Bastun's clearing" we know as Bassenthwaite. To a solitary islet on the bosom of Derwentwater came St. Herbert, to dwell alone in his hermit's cell; he prayed to God that he might die at the same time as his dearly loved friend, St. Cuthbert, and they did indeed die upon the same day, in A.D. 687. What happened in the next few centuries no one knows—Cumbria was part of Scotland at that period and the Norsemen had not yet come over the seas from Ireland and the Isle of Man to settle in the deep dales of Lakeland. They came in the tenth century and their place names are thick upon the map—Scandinavian names with an Irish flavour, many of them. Within the next century came the Norman Conquest and the gift of baronies to William's followers; the great barons in turn handed over large tracts of "wilderness" to the Church and the great abbeys round the fringe of Lakeland began to civilize them. At Crossfield, where Kentigern's cross had been planted, a new church was built in the twelfth century—the village was now called Crosthwaite—and pilgrims journeyed across Derwentwater to visit St. Herbert's Island; a small oratory was built there in the fourteenth century and after praying there the pilgrims bought little crucifixes, doubtless blessed by the priest, to take away as souvenirs. Their boats took them back to the Portinscale side of the lake, to Nichol End, where some time ago a small mould for making these mediæval crosses was found; it is now in the Keswick Museum, the repository of so many fascinating relics and finds relative to local history.

Keswick became used to visitors at an early period; they came and went. When an influx of German miners sanctioned by Queen Elizabeth arrived, and stayed, Keswick did not like it. In self-defence the foreigners settled on an island in the lake, built their homes, planted gardens and orchards, living peaceably—as they could not have done if they had attempted to dwell side by side with the natives. What life must have been like in Keswick in Tudor times is well portrayed in Hugh Walpole's novels, *Katharine Christian* and *Bright Pavilions.* No one has ever written so lovingly of the local scene as he did; his Herries Chronicle brings to life the eighteenth century too, in *Rogue Herries, Judith Paris* and *The Fortress.*

Two hundred years ago came the first curious travellers into Keswick Vale; some were artists, some poets, some just tourists. They stayed at one of the inns—of which there was good choice, for Keswick was now fairly prosperous with pack-horse traffic. There was the Queen's Head where Gray was "pretty well content" with his fare, the Royal Oak—called "Royal" after Charles the Second's restoration, and the King's Arms. The "Oak" later became the posting and coaching inn, the innkeeper having the office of postmaster also; when he retired he called his house the Acorn. The Oak was soon to be honoured by the great; a plaque to-day at its door tells of some of the lions who stayed there, Scott, Tennyson, Southey and Wordsworth and their friends among them.

There is so much literature to help one build up a picture of eighteenth-century Keswick and Borrowdale: Gray, Pennant, Young, Gilpin, West and Mrs. Radcliffe drew the scene in words, Devis and Farington on paper and canvas. The artists, like the writers, piled on the horrors at times; Farington's Cumbrian mountains are mighty Alps and his crags "impend awfully".

Gray saw Borrowdale with some trepidation. As he passed through the rock-strewn floor of the valley he was reminded of Alpine passes "where the guides tell you to move with speed and say nothing lest the agitation of the air should loosen the snows above and bring down a mass that would overwhelm a caravan". At Grange village, as he lunched at the farm—on butter, bowls of milk and oaten cakes, plus a cold tongue they had brought with them—he heard of the plundering of an eagle's eyrie. "All the dale are up in arms on such an occasion, for they lose abundance of lambs yearly, not to mention hares, partridge, grouse, etc." For utter sublimity and pastoral beauty he wandered along the margin of Derwentwater—and his "stations" are now almost all National Trust land. The pictures he saw through his perspective glass he said "would fairly sell for a thousand pounds" were an artist able to fix the colours in all their perfection.

A few years later West was minimizing the horrors of the countryside in his Guide. "Mr. Gray was so much intimidated with the accounts of Borrowdale that he proceeded no farther than Grange. But no such difficulties as he feared are now to be met with. The road is improved since his time, at least as far as necessary for anyone to proceed to see what is curious," he wrote, to soothe the fears of the intending tourist. Borrowdale, he added, was a little Eden, "its laborious inhabitants partaking of nothing of the ferocity of the country they live in". They were hospitable, civil and communicative and ought to be consulted by the stranger wishing to continue his Alpine journey over the pass heads to Wasdale or Langdale. "The shepherds only are conversant with the traditional annals of the mountains, and with all the secrets of the mysterious reign of chaos, and old Night; and they can only give proper information concerning their Arcana: for others, who live almost within the shadows of these mountains, are often ignorant of their names."

Wordsworth knew the same region. Derwentwater, he wrote, "was distinguished from all other lakes by being surrounded by sublimity; the fantastic mountains of Borrowdale to the south, the bold steeps of Wallow Crag and Lodore to the east". To Charles Lamb, at first a rather unwilling admirer of lake and mountain, the Keswick mountains were a network of "great floundering bears and monsters"—all couchant and asleep—and Skiddaw greatest of the "broad-breasted brethren".

He enjoyed his stay at Greta Hall and did all the usual things the first Lakers did and twentieth-century holiday-makers do. "We have clambered up to the top of Skiddaw, and I have waded up the bed of Lodore, in fine I have satisfied myself that there is such a thing as that which tourists call romantic, which I very much suspected before: they make such a spluttering about it, and toss their splendid epithets around them, till they give as dim a light as at four o'clock next morning the lamps do after an illumination." Lamb felt that this was a day "which would stand out like a mountain" in his life. Back in London he confessed he longed for the Lakes again. "You cannot conceive the degradation I felt at first from being accustomed to wander free as air among mountains, and bathe in rivers without being controlled by anyone, to come home and work. I felt very little, I had been dreaming I was a very great man. But that is going off——" The pleasures of Fleet Street were reasserting themselves once more.

Coleridge, when living with the Southeys at Greta Hall, never failed to delight in the cloud play, "the shapeless vapour on the mountains—the perpetual forms of Borrowdale" and, when he could, strode off into the mists which wreathed the peaks. Robert Southey on first living at Keswick realized at once that the mountains would inspire him—"The poet part of me will be fed and fostered here. I feel already in tune."

Shelley, honeymooning at the cottage on Chestnut Hill, overlooking the Vale of Keswick, saw the "gigantic mountains piled on each other—the million-tinted clouds—the lake smooth and black as polished jet", and cried, "Oh, these are sights attuneable to contemplation."

Six years later the young poet Keats entered Keswick from the Thirlmere road before breakfast on a June morning, eager to see everything of this enchanting country. He climbed Skiddaw—fortified by two glasses of the guide's rum—and felt the exhilaration which comes in climbing into the rarer air of the mountains. "All felt that elevation which a cold bath gives one. I felt as if I were going into a tournament." Poor Keats! He was going on to Scotland but his tour was to send him back to London "with Death in his throat".

A few months after his return south he was writing *Hyperion*. He had before him memories of June and "fagging up hill at the end of a long, happy day", to see "those aged stones on a gentle rise in the midst of the mountains". The circle on Castlerigg found its place in the poem:

"——a dismal cirque
Of druid stones upon a forlorn moor."

Not only poets broke into verse inspired by the Keswick scene. In the Museum, verses are added to the maps made by Peter Crosthwaite, whose own Museum was founded in Keswick in 1789. He was obviously very pleased with his muse. To-day his lines we find very comic. For a taste:

"Here's Beauty, Grandeur and Magnificence in Piles!"

Or, to encourage the not-so-wealthy tourist:

> " An Earthly Paradise, a Feast for every sense
> This Northern Tour affords (and health) at small expense."

Of these artists and writers the more honest ones were restrained and less prone to indulge in the "horrors", or to throw their "spluttering and splendid epithets" about. Others, like Mrs. Radcliffe, whose *Mysteries of Udolpho* so impressed the heroine of Northanger Abbey, let themselves go and piled up the agonies of Borrowdale, where "mountains of granite shook into almost every possible form of horror". All around

CASTLERIGG CIRCLE

Keswick, they assured their stay-at-home friends and correspondents, was nothing but " Beauty in the lap of Horror "; and their friends doubtless believed them.

But now, how many arm-chaired travellers doing their Seven Lakes Tour bat an eyelid as they cruise comfortably down the Borrowdale road? Not one. The Cumbrian mountains have shrunk considerably in the last two centuries. After Switzerland, Cumberland seems small; the youth hostellers who climb the Stake and the Sty possibly walked last year in the Alps. The motor-coach full of tourists is probably returning from a seven-day tour of Scotland, and to their eyes these are but small hills. Nevertheless, many among them see this valley for what it is; size is not Lakeland's claim to be placed high among the beautiful regions of Britain; exquisite proportion, infinite variety of form and colour, and an atmosphere of enchantment—these are her chief attributes. When the Wordsworths and Coleridge returned from their Scottish tour in the autumn of 1803 Dorothy could not answer the question, whether the Scottish or English lakes were the more beautiful—"no comparison can be made where everything is different . . . certainly nothing is so beautiful in Scotland as in parts of this country". And Coleridge, answering the same question, said, "intervals between the fine things in Scotland are very dreary, whereas in Cumberland and Westmorland is a cabinet of beauties—each thing being beautiful in itself—the very passage of one lake, mountain or valley to another is itself a beautiful thing again".

Ambleside and Keswick thrived as market towns because they were such good centres, the very reason which sends twentieth-century tourists flocking there. "Such good centres—and so handy for the buses and tours," they say. Round Tours: Keswick excels in them—the Ullswater Round, the Bassenthwaite Round, and that most beautiful journey along Buttermere and Crummack Water which West wrote of as a ride "which remains hitherto unnoticed though one of the most pleasing and surprising in the environs of Keswick . . . through some of the finest, solemn pastoral scenes the tourist has yet beheld". From the Pass of Newlands he declared: "Whoever would enjoy, with ease and safety, Alpine views and pastoral scenes in the sublime style may have them in this morning ride." He soothed the fears of the timorous. "No villainous banditti haunt the mountains; innocent people live in the dells . . . mountain virtue and pastoral hospitality are found in every farm." He directed the notice of the Visitor of Taste to the "natural elegance" displayed in the valleys, where "every dalelander appears to be a man of taste and every village, house and cot is placed in the choicest site and decorated in the neatest manner . . ."

Compare this with the language chosen by modern Tour boosters. With a great deal of ingenuity the motor-coach proprietors devise their five—seven—and even eleven lakes tours; very few dwellers in the Lancashire and Yorkshire industrial towns have not at some time enjoyed one or other of the trips, to many a first introduction to the Lakes. If it encourages them to come again intending to savour the pleasures more slowly it is a good thing; if they merely remain content to see the Lakes again behind glass it is not so good. And if they insist on having with them their children, bringing them up to think the height of felicity is to do the seven or eleven lakes tour in a "chara"—then it is a sad and a bad thing.

Coach companies do not run their tours in the off-seasons. So to recapture the joys of the open road, as earlier travellers tasted them, the Keswick country is best seen in the quiet times—in February for instance. Among my most memorable visits was one Shrovetide when I seized the opportunity of a few days among the mountains. The fact that the mountains were under snow made it more memorable; snowfalls transformed the landscape into something rich and strange. Blizzards on the tops renewed in me a deep respect for the mountains; mist and clouds have often baffled us in path-finding, but blinding snow was a new experience.

Coming north the sun shone, the sky was blue; there was an almost April blandness in the air over Windermere. On Dunmail Raise we passed through banks of snow cut by roadmen after earlier drifts; at the road edge piles labelled GRIT were there for the convenience of road-users when ice gripped the surface. Thirlmere was silent as the tomb; no wind blew, no water moved; in the gills were icicles, the lake was frozen, black ice save where eddies of snow had blown across it or where chill green water lapped in little waves over submerged packs. At Legburthwaite a farmer driving little Swaledales along before him shouted, "More snaw on t' way," but seeing the rift of St. John's Vale, with the visionary splendour of Skiddaw and Saddleback, gleaming white in sun, pure cobalt in shade, framed therein—and looking on Derwentwater later, dream-like under dreaming mountains, I thought little of his warning.

Winter offers wonderful experiences in Cumberland—and strange contrasts. Along Derwentwater shore, not far beyond Friars Crag, I found a sheltered spot by the twisted roots of conifers. The sun shone, the lake—unfrozen—delicately tinted as mother-o'-pearl—rippled about the rocks. One boatman was on the lake—he and his boat in silhouette. Seagulls screamed; silence fell. A pair of mallard passed over, neck and neck. Again a stillness—not of this earth. I waited; out of the silence grew a strange sound—a song, yet hardly a song, a singing, whirring, stringed instrument sound. Down the lake came a white bird, a wild swan, with neck outstretched, winging its way north; its wing-song grew fainter and became part of the silence. The day was drawing to a close. Sunlight slanted into the Jaws of Borrowdale, spilling upon the rocks and crags which were so "horrific" to the first visitors. Never have I seen a view less horrific. The lake sparkled into life, gold light touched the wavelets, gold outlined the frosty branches, the enchanted circle of mountains changed from clear, chalky blue to deeper hues, then paled to hyacinth as the sun went down. Such an evening, I thought, promised a soft day to follow.

The next morning—Sunday—snow was falling. A roadman, busy sweeping the night's fall with a long broom, told me the wind was "backening into t'west" and he believed there'd be more snow before we had finished with it. On which words I pondered on my way to Matins at Crosthwaite church. In the churchyard snowdrops and crocuses valiantly pushed their heads through the snow. Mine was the first foot printed on the path to Southey's grave. The congregation do not come this way on a cold morning; they proceed into the church and wait in the warmth whilst from the ringing chamber on the ground floor of the west tower the ringers pull manfully. The valley and the mountains hear St. Kentigern's bells more clearly than we within the church.

At eleven-thirty, when the congregation went homeward, I turned to Portinscale. The snow was over, fitful gleams of sun travelled over the whiteness of Catbells. At Swinside the air was milder, but Newlands was invisible in the thrall of wilder elements. The Ice King and the Snow Queen were there; none was to be allowed near the place where they held conclave. Borrowdale was more inviting, or at least not repellent. I trod a smooth white path along the slope of Catbells; it was good walking, the snow crunchy and firm. I could cast my eyes over all the heights east and west; all were white giants, but woods, copses, and the straggling walls—they were black or brown, clearly drawn upon the whiteness. The lake, so lovely yesterday, was to-day a steely, grey-blue shield. When I came to the double-arched bridge at Grange-in-Borrowdale I heard the shouts of boys skating, tracing patterns on smooth ice. Up-river the unfrozen pools of the Derwent were the deepest turquoise under the delicate white tracery of birches.

I was tempted updale, up the old lane the eighteenth-century travellers knew as their highroad to the Bowder Stone—the scene here impressive in the extreme. Standing there I became conscious of a change in the wind's voice. When a farmer passed —he was bringing sheep in from Grange Fell—and called in passing, "It's wild up yonder," glancing to the fell, I should have been warned. The wind was howling now; I could hear it from the comparative shelter of the crags. Nevertheless I decided to go over the tops to Watendlath. I knew all the paths there, but a short cut I did not know would take me—according to my map

—in a very short time into the next dale. I had the strongest desire to see Watendlath in just such wintry conditions the day offered.

There was a stile at the road edge with a thin path climbing to a wall gap. I reached the gap and found the way continued, slippery and steep, above a birch wood. At higher level it lost itself under glass-smooth ice—but on I went. Suddenly, round huge, grey boulders, a gale rushed at me, with a noise like a pack of belling hounds. Snow came with it, a few flakes at first, then more and more until I was cut off from the world by a dizzy, whirling blizzard. An eerie snow silence fell. Feeling sure I was near the ridge and would soon look down to the Watendlath valley and there take my bearings if the tarn showed, I plodded on into deeper snow. But on the tops was a welter of rocks, so many, all alike, with tiny hollows between them and all with smooth thread-like paths going off in all directions. When I thought I had reached the top I could see nothing—no dale, no tarn, no farms, only dark rocks falling away before me—and, through a sudden rent in the white pall, what I saw was surely the Bowder Stone gill and a small area of grey which looked suspiciously like Derwentwater. In all other directions was snow, blowing like white smoke.

In my own footprints, not yet obliterated, I retraced my way back to the birches, the wall gap and the road-side stile.

I could look at my map again. Hardly any snow was falling in the dale bottom. Where had my path-finding gone wrong? Not many yards ahead of my false start I found the perfectly foolproof track plainly waymarked "WATENDLATH". The afternoon was still young. I set off again, hopefully, for soon I knew I would come to the familiar Rosthwaite track. There I could not lose my way however wild the storm might blow.

I trudged upwards, from the deep lane with its boulder-piled walls, to the bracken slopes—memories of blazing autumn—to the six tall trees sentinel by the higher track—memories of summer, and long rests here to gaze upon the almost overwhelming loveliness of the Borrowdale bowl drowsy beneath blue skies and purple mountains—to the larch wood—memories of a cuckoo shouting his name to the dales and the green veil of April—to the stony descent upon Watendlath hamlet. The snow was crunchy underfoot, but my mind was playing with thoughts of hot days, with hay-timing which makes so gay a pattern of the valley floor about the tarn, with thoughts of the mirror-like blueness of the tarn itself and the white ducks paddling about its marge. Then I returned to winter with a start. The tarn was not there at all. I looked again. A patch of white, smooth as a tablecloth—that was the tarn, its ice mantled by snow.

As I looked down the whiteness turned to the palest pink. The sky was suffused with a rosy sunset flush—the mountain-tops catching it were touched with an Alpine glow.

Rarely have I been so deeply moved on any of my many descents upon Watendlath. The tiny community gripped within

FARM AT WATENDLATH

the knees of the high fells was itself at this hour, at this season. As in the Middle Ages, when abbey tenants cared for abbey flocks, its sole concern was sheep farming; tourists, catering, borrowing romance from the Herries novels, luring visitors with the names of Judith Paris and John Green—none of these concerned the place at all.

I came into Watendlath in the dusk when the whiteness of the snowy land made daylight linger. All were indoors and no dog barked. No one expected visitors or had doors open to travellers. I found the farm with a phone. This was good. Friends in Keswick would be starting to worry.

"Can I use the phone?" I was taken into a dark passage, groped after a girl into a darker room with only a little light given by a dying fire. There was the phone—I felt for the receiver. People moved in the darkness. No one made any attempt to light lamps. I felt for my purse; fingered the edges of coins for pennies, found them and, thanking the invisible inhabitants for their courtesy, stumbled out over a stone passage into the porch. The door framed a dark tree, a wedge of fell, a sapphire sky and the evening star. Living in towns has spoilt us for the simplicities of life in the country.

Leaving Watendlath, plodding through deep snow few other feet had flattened for me, I thought on these things. We shall have to think of them more and more. How can Borrowdale enjoy the blessings of electricity and yet retain its unspoilt landscape? By underground cables? A start has been made.

I trudged on. I had five miles for deep meditation. The sky turned to dark blue—then to grey-green—out came the seven lucky stars—then galaxies of stars and the Milky Way. Once came an eerie owl-like sound, a sudden whimper, a squeal. I heard the roaring of waters down Lodore and strange gurglings of becks beneath ice. Far away appeared fallen stars; lights from Keswick. Several times I had frozen gate catches to struggle with. A sudden shuffling noise came from an Ashness barn.

Rather bold, I made my way to the edge of the great crags; in summer one sits with a tree for back rest and idly considers the blueness of Derwentwater and the minute boats upon it so very far and away below. I withdrew quickly; a frightening pit seemed to yawn below.

Ashness Bridge—a freezing stillness—a thin trickling sound only from the beck. Ahead a reeling form—a Watendlath farmer homeward bound?

"Road's bad below," he said. "Shot ice."

From the house of friends on Chestnut Hill the lake that night looked like the Bay of Naples, with Skiddaw, monstrous, velvety black against the icy glitter of stars.

Note well: "Most Beautiful Road" is in quotes. Is it quite as beautiful nowadays? A591 as a major road is excellent, with every attempt to harmonise with the glorious landscape: lay-bys, picnic spots with lovely prospects, and alternative pedestrian paths alongside. Commerce, trade, and the tourist traffic flow along freely.

The pity is that major roads in scale with the Alps and the Rockies are not right in our Cumbrian mountains. I would like to hear Father West, Wordsworth and Ruskin discussing this "on the other side of the grave".

IV

KESWICK TO PENRITH

HIGHWAYS AND BYWAYS

From Troutbeck to Matterdale and Ullswater

Ullswater Ways—Glenridding, Grisedale, Patterdale and Hartsop

Mountain Ways—into Bannerdale and Martindale

Paths to Pooley Bridge—from Howtown, Moor Divock

Eamont Valley villages—Dacre, Barton, Sockbridge, Tirril, Yanwath to Eamont Bridge

Journey's End

KESWICK TO PENRITH—BY WAY OF ULLSWATER

PENRITH is but eighteen miles from Keswick, but in some ways they are worlds apart. When Keswick was an outpost among the mountains, home of hardly civilized boors, Penrith was on one of the highroads of English and Scottish history, a front-line town which had time and time again withstood the rigours of border warfare. Penrith is at the edge of the lowlands, rich, low and fruitful country about it, with hay and cornfields upon which the sun shines when the Borrowdale mountains are darkened by a scowl of clouds. How many times have we trudged back to Keswick soaked by August rains on the Sty or Greenup Edge or Honister Pass, only to meet friends who spent the day shopping in Penrith in pleasant sunny weather!

A modern bus takes us in an hour from Keswick to Penrith, through Threlkeld, Scales and Liscow, through the farmlands under the mountain wall of Blencathra and Souter Fell, by the Glenderamakin River, over open country to Penruddock, Keldhead and Red Hills—or roundabout through Greystoke, a village with ancient church and a castle once the seat of the Barons of Greystoke. Pleasant and uneventful taken from west to east, this journey going westwards in the evening against the setting sun can be charged with magic. I have seen the mountains wax larger and larger beyond Troutbeck, giants crowding into the sky, turning from lilac to deepest purple, to fade after the last spate of flame and fire into the evening blueness. I can well understand folk imagining strange apparitions under such conditions. Souter Fell has more than once played background for ghostly cavalcades.

Many old travel-writers tell of what men reported they had seen in 1735, 1737, in 1745 and 1774—and usually on Midsummer Eve. One saw troops crossing Souter Fell, and two years later marching soldiers were seen again; in 1745 the spectacle of men and carriages of ammunition crossing the mountains was so real to the watchers that they climbed the slopes to find their footprints—and found nothing. From the north came news of Jacobite troops manœuvring—in fact—after which some declared the sights on Souter were no more than mirages. Thirty years later the armies were marching again, on steep slopes where no horse could tread—yet many folk beheld them for two hours and more.

The main highway to Penrith is well enough—but not for walking. I found a much better route, across country, from Penruddock through the parkland about Hutton John, Dacre Castle and Dalemain, to Barton church and Sockbridge—green paths and grassy lanes all the way. If roads must be used, then let the way to Penrith be by Matterdale, Ullswater and the Eamont Valley.

One August morning torrential rains prevented me from walking to Matterdale from Birkett Bank—in St. John's Vale—to Dockray. The same happened once before, during a very wild September.

This route is one "recommended" by local people to walkers who find, through mist and snow, that the Sticks Pass is not advisable as a way to reach Ullswater and Patterdale. Eighteenth-century travellers took the precaution of hiring local guides—not having the good maps we use—when going across Matterdale Common. William and Dorothy Wordsworth came this way when going to visit their friends at Hallsteads and Dacre; Dorothy writes in her journal of a December journey in snow, of the "dreary bare hills, the cold and slippery track', the hail-storms, and how "the hills looked large and swelling through the storm". How glad they were to reach the inn at Matterdale, to crowd near the fire, to eat "porridge and Christmas pies"!

MATTERDALE CHURCH

The dalefolk I consulted insisted that the track was not one to take in bad weather, for wartime usage had broken up the surface and the boggy nature of the common had completed the damage, so I caught the bus to Troutbeck Station, by which time the weather had relented and all was set for a good day. A party of climbers at the door of the old inn (it has a 1680 date over it) faced Saddleback and sunlit slopes; I had the long, straight road ahead of me and time to take in all the details of the great stretch of open country—a farmer whistling to his dog on Great Mell Fell—one of the twin conical hills which rise from the level plateau, each a volcanic plug—where his flocks were being rounded up for the sheep dipping. I looked behind me at the Skiddaw massif, and forward to the sky-line over which other ranges were beginning to peep, one after the other, the Westmorland heights beyond Ullswater, until at the dale head of Matterdale the entire and glorious regiment of giants was lined up to the east.

After the very bare and treeless uplands Matterdale was a lovely, cosy, green hollow holding summer in its arms; wild roses grew there still, raspberries were ripe in the hedges and purple vetch trailed among the thorns; small grey farms scattered among the hills had each the pattern of hay-timing about them—fields, dark green, pale emerald and yellow—and to bring variety each had its own grovelet of pines or larches. Green paths wandered about the tilted pastures; some came to the dale and converged upon the lowly church. How very satisfying are all these Cumbrian churches in the mountains, lowly, crude, unassuming, and because of their rough-hewn masonry showing very few traces of old age. This house of God was built in the days of Elizabeth I, after the dalesfolk had petitioned for a church of their own, the mother church—Greystoke—being far away and difficult to reach in wild weather. They were granted their church, which they built in the 1570's; it has simple barn-like construction, the heavy beam nearest the chancel end being carved with numerals which are somewhat puzzling. MdXX $^{\text{xxx}}_{\text{xxiii}}$—does this stand for 1573, seven years after the date of the appeal to the Queen, or is it 1753, a later carving upon an original part of the roofing? The oldest object in the church is without doubt the font, a bowl of red sandstone which originally belonged to the mother church at Greystoke. It has passed through many vicissitudes, being used as a cheese-press stone in a Dockray farm, then as the base of a sun-dial before it was returned to the place where it was intended. The pulpit is a perfect example of north-country Jacobean. It is hinted that at one time the Communion wine for the church was kept in this pulpit, in a wooden keg which had contained more potent spirits.

According to church records a number of repairs and alterations were completed in 1750 (the beam carving might well be the work of the carpenters who did the work), after which new seats had to be fairly allocated and lots were cast, eight seats at the "bell end" to be reserved for the singers and "a seat in the alleyway near the pulpit to be for the use of the old men and for such as cannot hear well". I can picture the patriarchs of the dale with their white beards, and hands cupping their ears, intent on the wise saws of the eighteenth-century parson as he leaned on the edge of the same pulpit.

From the cool interior I stepped out into the churchyard, wandering from grave to grave and finding two interesting stone slabs among them—one in memory of Margaret, wife of Edward Dawson, bonesetter—a beautiful tablet, and the other in memory of the same Edward who died in 1747.

"Remember to keep holy the Lord's Day,
On it refrain from drinking and from play"—

the play referred possibly to the hunt—Matterdale men, like those Troutbeck and Caldbeck way, were great after the fox.

There is a very old story which shows of what mettle Matterdale folk were made long ago. Matterdale men were fighters for the right, upholders of Justice. In 1639 the common grazing rights enjoyed by them and by their forbears generations before them were threatened. Lesser men would have given them up without protest. In the fight they "spent half their estates, and one man walked to London in three days in his wooden clogs" to give evidence at the lawsuit—and it was won for the farmers of Matterdale. Three hundred miles in three days on two feet? Matterdale men must have been wonderful walkers too—or wonderful tellers of tall stories. Three weeks, surely.

From the church to the road again, past Hollows (called "Hollas") Farm which has its old wood-pegged door and a brewhouse, relic of the days when this was a much-frequented wayside inn. There was another inn lower down the dale at Dockray, the likely place of call for the Wordsworths, a public house then kept by a landlady with a handsome husband and "little Jewish daughters", the husband going a mile and a half along the road to show the travellers their way to Mr. Clarkson's house near Pooley Bridge.

To-day Dockray looked quite enchanting in the sunshine, with the Aira glancing and singing over its stones, and bouts of scent coming from the cottage gardens. I passed the inn and the hotel but opened a garden gate and, at the end of a long path flanked by clipped yews and rose bushes, came to a cottage where I lunched within sound of a rippling beck and birds singing. An hour later, going on towards Ullswater, I entered the National Trust estate, including Aira Force and Gowbarrow Park—the familiar oak leaf sign is the only indication—and I was gazing at last, enraptured, on the middle reaches of the lake, hardly knowing what in the enchanting scene was reality and which reflection, the lake so faithfully repeats the multi-coloured flanks

ULLSWATER SHORE—NEAR SANDWICK

of overshadowing fells and mountains. I had forgotten that the vision of Ullswater could be quite so breath-takingly beautiful—and that the woods below with their green glades and aged trees were so very near to Faery. Here I have been fortunate enough to see the deer in the early morning. The " fallow deer glancing about the lawns and bounding through the thickets " were among the attractions of the Park in Wordsworth's time; in his Guide he writes " here the lover of Nature might linger for hours . . . here is a powerful brook which dashes among rocks through a deep glen . . . here beds of luxurious fern, aged hawthorns and hollies decked with honeysuckle . . . these the attractions of the retired view, or foreground for ever-varying pictures of the majestic lake . . ."

In the list of National Trust properties in the Lake District this "most romantic of Parks", "this place romantic, sublime, enchanted"—to quote early tourists—is described briefly as "750 acres, mainly fell, with many footpaths, wooded glen with specimen trees and waterfall, tea house at Aira Green . . . red and fallow deer". How cold and bare the facts! How enchanting the reality! "Slip thou away," wrote Christopher North, "down into the dell and, sound-led, ascend in music deeper and deeper still towards Airey Force, that like a continuous succession of small avalanches, keeps tumbling for ever into 'liquid lapses' that sing their way to the lake through heaven-hiding woods." To-day, as I saw the glen, the enchantment remained, in spite of the tourists who came climbing along the narrow paths and lined up on the bridges. Once it was a dangerous place to wander in, by day, or sleep-walking like "The Somnambulist" of the poem.

From the upper bridge we saw a spout of amber water leap and rebound from a water-smoothed rock wall, to wear away, by constant water-drops, another, then plunge away into a deep abyss. The lower bridge is wet with continual spray from other falls. The path drops to lower levels, under rocks where harebells sway in the falling spray and drooping ferns and cushions of green moss alike are patterned with diamond droplets. Then the glen opens wider, the beck flows placidly into a woodland full of damp earthy scents and under-water green light. And soon we pass into the sun—and there is the Car Park, the motor-coaches and the Tea House. Nothing inaccessible about this beauty spot now.

The eighteenth-century "discoverers" of Ullswater were loud in their praises. For a taste take West:

> "The accompaniments of this lake are disposed in the most picturesque order, bending round its margin, and spreading upwards in craggy rocks and mountains, irregular in outline; yet they are certainly much inferior in sublimity and horrible grandeur to the environs of Keswick, and the dreadful rocks in Borrowdale."

Sweet, pleasing, delightful, charming, describe the scene for West, and he is pleased to tell his readers of an agreeable diversion likely to be afforded them as they tour along the lake. He quotes from Mr. Hutchinson's *Excursion to the Lakes.*

> "Whilst we sat to regale, a barge put off from shore to a

station where the finest echoes were to be obtained from the surrounding mountains. The vessel was provided with six brass cannons mounted on swivels—on discharging one of these pieces the report was echoed from the opposite rocks, whereby reverberations seemed to roll from cliff to cliff and return through every cave and valley, till the decreasing tumult gradually died away upon the ear."

To the wonder of all who watched and listened the report of every discharge "was re-echoed seven times distinctly". I think we hear enough reports from backfiring cars as they climb the hill to Matterdale. We prefer the sound of "lake waters lapping on the shore".

Was the first poet to "tune his lyre" in honour of this enchanting lake the oft-quoted Mr. Cumberland?—whose *Ode to the Sun* was known to many of the early travellers. According to West he toured the Lakes at a wet season—so familiar two centuries later—and saw little besides "weeping rocks, flooded roads and watery plains darkened by sable clouds" until he reached the shores of Ullswater. And there, behold, the clouds broke, the light poured down and in praise of the sun he wrote his ode.

"But see the embattled vapours break,
Disperse and fly,
Posting like couriers down the sky;
The grey rock glitters in the glassy lake;
And now the mountain-tops are seen
Frowning amidst the blue serene;
The variegated groves appear,
Deckt in the colours of the waning year."

Gazing on the scene of enchantment he offered the palm to this lake and dale.

"Imperial lake of Patrick's dale:
For neither Scottish lowlands pride,
Nor smooth Killarney's silver tide,
Nor ought that learned Poussin drew
Or dashing Rosa flung upon my view,
Shall shake thy sovreign, undisturbed right,
Great scene of wonder and sublime delight."

What a pity Thomas Gray saw the lake on a dull October day

without a gleam of sunshine. One gleam, and the difference it would have made! Late autumn can be the most glorious of all seasons by Ullswater; in October and November I have been dazed with the colour and beauty. But I am writing of the high summer pomps, and autumn gold on this landscape must wait.

From Matterdale road end to Patterdale, six delightful miles, there is nothing between the road and the waves but the grey shingle and the bushes—yes, and if you come at the lucky season, daffodils dancing as Dorothy Wordsworth saw them one March day in 1802 below Gowbarrow Park, tossed about by the wind which blew upon them over the lake. There are a score of dallying spots in a mile, convenient boulders to sit upon, little wavelets lapping at our feet, mossy banks and bared tree roots shaped like rustic benches, and always the changing hues and forms of the fells above Martindale, Boardale and Bannerdale. I have stayed so often at farms along this shore and wandered so many times among the dales and fells on the far side that even when I sit quite still my memory and my imagination are wandering in among them.

Before the War, when we walked in the hills across the lake, we found it a minor Eden, a little Paradise, remote country to dream about when we returned to town. During the War we were locked out, for the Martindale area was an army training ground. When it was freed we enjoyed roaming in these outback dales all the more.

Cars and buses go by, bound for Pooley Bridge and Penrith by way of Watermillock, Tirril and Yanwath—a beautiful road to travel. I shall make my way to Pooley Bridge roundabout and through the fells of Martindale. But first I must climb the lane to the vale of Glenridding, where I shall stay the night.

It was evening by the time I reached Greenside, the Youth Hostel which now occupies the old mine office buildings at the head of Glenridding, one of the mountain base hostels so popular with mountaineers—like the Copper Mines hostel above Coniston —for the climbing begins almost from the back door. To most of us these mines are nothing but an eyesore, a blot on the landscape, and a pollution to the water, so it was interesting to talk to the miners of their work and to learn of attempts to cover the ugly places. The road to the hostel is a steep and stony one climbing to the north of a mountain stream, passing rows of miners' cottages—some a hundred years old—where dwell families for generations employed under the great mass of Helvellyn, as miners, experiencing bad times and good. Now, several elderly men told me, there was very little lead left and final closure not long away. The last lean times were in the 1930's when the mines were closed and men on relief three and four years—but, as miners are adaptable, some were able to find other jobs, farming, coal-mining. One old man, his hands and fingers twisted with years of shovel work, knew mining conditions up at Nent Head, on the high Pennines above High Cup Nick, where every miner is a small-holder too—"and what better—fresh air nivver comes amiss after hours down below, and change of exercise is as good as a rest". One man called Dewis remembered when the lead was smelted here too and ingots were sent away stamped GREENSIDE; nowadays the lead was crushed—Billy Hicks was in charge of the crushing plant—and then sent away to Newcastle or Chester to be smelted, the same company owning mines in the Halkyn Mountain of North Wales having various works for their minerals. We talked on a bridge just above the hostel where the gill is a desolate rocky place, the stream bed full of tumbled boulders and all is confusion. About 1923 the dam of the tarn high in Helvellyn, Keppel Cove, burst; a tremendous rush of water swept down the gill, tearing away the rocks, leaving all this as a witness of the destruction. Near by were other outward signs of inward and hidden work going on within the mountain. The mine goes one mile into the earth, then 90 fathoms down, proceeds another half-mile and then drops 50 fathoms, so the men working at the end had quite a long journey; pit ponies stabled down in the village used to carry the men and do hauling down below, but they were then replaced by "little locos". In the war over three hundred men worked here; in 1948 about eighty. But now the mines are closed and many miners' cottages are owned by weekenders.

All this was very interesting. One man told me of the latest attempts to cover up the hideous waste—and there is a considerable amount from lead mines. A long, grey, lifeless slope above the gill had for years taken tons of waste. Now it was pumped along the mountainside—formerly pony-drawn trucks tipped it there—lime floated over it and, a most noble effort, grass sown upon it with the hopes that the grey would become green and ugliness no longer shriek from Glenridding.

"You see, yon lime's spread on to bind waste together. Then grass blades ought to bind lot—but it has to be Blackpool grass, sort that you get on them sandhills—sort they planted to stop erosion—and if sheep don't start feeding from off mountain it ought to be green as a meadow in a few years. But I reckon it'll take a live wire to keep sheep off." So one of the Glenridding miners said, and his companion nodded agreement. I hoped the grass-growing would succeed. Glenridding ought to be as fair as the sister dales of Matterdale, Glencoyne, Grisedale and Deepdale; there ought to be no ugly sister in the Ullswater family.

No fewer than twelve sister becks and dales pay tribute to Ullswater and each one has her own attributes of beauty; Aira Beck from Matterdale, the becks from Glencoyne and Glenridding, and Grisedale, Deepdale, Dovedale and Caudale which all meet in Patterdale, and Hartsop too—the hope or valley of the hart; Boardale, Bannerdale, Ramsgill, Fusedale are the deep valleys of Martindale Forest running to the lake from the Westmorland mountains. Matterdale brought the road from Keswick to the lake, but Glencoyne has no road, only a track to the old farm which backs into the wooded slopes and seems as natural a growth as the trees themselves. Hound puppies run down the lane to meet a stranger. Later they will be trained to hunt with the famous Ullswater pack. Glenridding takes its waters from "mighty Helvellyn", from Keppel Cove and Red Tarn, and its milky stream carries pollution into the lake. The dale has still its emerald pastures and threading footpaths—I used them in coming down to Patterdale after my night at Greenside. Grisedale—where swine were turned out in the olden days—is the way down from the high pass, from St. Sunday Crag and Fairfield, and from the lone tarn below Grisedale Hause; down this path came young John Wordsworth, the poet's brother, in 1805, after a leave-taking at the brink of the tarn where he loved to spend quiet hours fishing. The leave-taking was the last the brothers made there; soon afterwards the "sailor brother" was to be drowned at sea. In lightly falling snow in April 1805 a young man called Gough came up from Patterdale with a little yellow-haired bitch at heel; their passing was hardly noticed yet they become immortalized. Three months later newspapers reported the finding of his bones near Red Tarn and the fidelity of the little dog watching his master's remains fired the imagination of at least two poets. Both Scott and Wordsworth visited the sad spot where the wanderer died.

How familiar the opening lines are!

> "A barking sound the shepherd hears,
> A cry as of a dog or fox——"

and in Scott's best style:

> "I climbed the dark brow of the mighty Helvellyn,
> Lakes and mountains beneath me gleamed misty and
> wide——"

Though no poets record such tragedies nowadays, Patterdale talks of happenings which Wordsworth, did he live now, might tell in verse. For instance when I was at Kirkstone in 1948 there was much talk about the dramatic rescue of Butcher, a terrier, which had gone to earth in a vixen's borran and remained there, incarcerated for no less than fourteen days, during which time nineteen Patterdale men never relaxed their efforts to free her. They sold picture postcards of the "lile terrier" in the shops and the men were rewarded by the R.S.P.C.A. In 1951 when I stayed in Patterdale there was a sadness over the valley, for everyone remembered too clearly the tragedies of Easter. Two girls left a youth hostel to cross the Fairfield ridges. When they were later reported to be missing, the snow blizzards which had swept over the mountains prevented searchers from finding their tracks. Their bodies were found not far from each other on the side of Deepdale, not so very far from the valley floor. Their deaths, and that of a man the same week-end on the far side of the same mountains made people realize that the mountains must be respected. In bad weather they can be very cruel. There will always be walkers who ignore good advice.

The National Trust Handbook is right in saying "the fells should be approached with a certain humility and respect, and the crags more so—they are never to be trifled with, and in storm and cloud and darkness they can be very dangerous indeed——". Exposure—too light clothing—can cause death just as a fall can.

Whilst on the subject of mountain crossings I should mention a true story told to me by one whose family hailed from a hamlet at the head of Patterdale. A small boy of seven or eight years old was sent off to visit a relative at Gatesgarth near Buttermere. His father gave him instructions, saw him safely to the head of Grisedale, pointed the route he must take over the fells from Thirlmere to Watendlath, told him that at Rosthwaite he must ask directions for the rest of the way—to Seatoller and Honister Pass—and there left him to trudge alone, manfully, through the heart of Lakeland. He reached Gatesgarth safely. I wonder how many fond parents to-day would trust their offspring to the mercy of the fells at so tender an age?

Where Grisedale Beck hastens through a wooded valley to Patterdale is the Hall of Marshalls and Mounseys. The dale is "laid out" here with landscape gardening, avenues and paths by lovely cascades, work planned by the first Marshalls, who were greatly interested in tree planting. They succeeded in 1824 to the estates of the Mounseys who "from time immemorial" had ruled as kings in Patterdale—some said from the date of a great victory against Scots Raiders in the narrow gap between Stybarrow Crag and the lake edge, when the local dalesmen were led by the Mounsey of the period. There must have been many Mounseys who were characters—Patterdale was rather proud of them—among whom the eighteenth-century "King" was surely the oddest. He was exceedingly close-fisted with his money and used all his strength—which was considerable—to save expense. He used to row one of his own boats down the lake to Pooley Bridge, laden with slates and timber, which he sold at the best prices in the market. When at home he laboured like a navvy, patched his stocking heels with leather to save wear and tear, wore the usual dalesman's wooden-soled clogs shod with iron, borrowed his tenants' best suits when he needed to look respectable, demanded the feudal right of meals in tenants' homes, slept at night under hedges and in barns when travelling because he was too miserly to stay at an inn, and he constantly worried himself with the fear of being robbed. The Patterdale folk, knowing his habit of hiding his wealth in holes and wall crannies, were always hopeful of finding some of "the old man's brass"! When he died at the age of ninety-two he left the old hall so sadly neglected that his son finally sold the estates and Mounseys were seen no more in the dale.

There are some who like to think that Patterdale is dedicated to the Irish saint who came, they say, over the mountains in the fifth century and baptized the natives at a spring of water by the lakeside—the well dubbed St. Patrick's to-day. The little church is St. Patrick's—a modern church on an older site, a simple chapel in the mountains, the only one to serve all the dalesfolk between Kirkstone Pass and Watermillock. Patterdale is a complete village with school, hotels, boarding houses, shops—with a modern mini-market, and a post office-general store which has a notice board telling of local events, fixtures and "do's" in such number that a stranger from town who thinks country life is dull must be surprised when he reads the list. Perhaps the autumn and winter programme is the fullest, when the visitors have gone and the villagers can enjoy their own recreations—

Football Matches, Football Socials, Hot-Pot Suppers, a Barn Dance, a Grand Concert, W.E.A. lectures on local history by the vicar, etc., etc.

I like to visit centres like Patterdale and Grasmere in the "off season", if only to see them in their old guise. In such places there is welcome too, but in very limited quantity. Hotels and houses employing large staffs close down when the season ends; the family-run guest houses and smaller hotels only are open. In November, darkness drawing on, I walked many miles along the lake road calling at no fewer than five doors asking for the night a resting place. At one they were going off to the Hunt Ball at Keswick, at the next they had no staff, at the third the decorators were in—and so on. Finally I was compelled to walk back to Pooley Bridge and was immediately provided with all I wanted at the Sun. So—tourists be warned. between October and Easter.

Now for a roundabout approach to Penrith, into the mountains and through the dales on the east and Westmorland side of Ullswater.

> "Go travel 'mid the hills. There tuneful streams
> Are touching myriad stops invisible;
> And winds and leaves and birds and your own thoughts
> (Not the least glad) in wordless chorus crowd
> Around the thymele of Nature."

So it is with us when we seek the quietude of the country hidden away behind Place Fell—"peace waits among the hills".

Goldrill Beck threads the green floor of the upper dale between Ullswater and Brothers Water, the road to Kirkstone on the west of it, and on the lower slopes of the fells to the east a delightful track linking farm after farm with the ancient community of Low Hartsop. To reach this old road Goldrill Bridge is crossed, just beyond the village of Patterdale. Now we can forget all about roads and motor-coaches for many happy hours. Over the bridge two or three cottages are grouped at the fork of the lanes. One which faces updale and watches the old track is "Wordsworth's Cottage". Miss Ann Macbeth, the artist and maker of the lovely embroideries and tapestries in Patterdale church, lived here until her death in 1948. In 1805 it was the home of friends of the Wordsworths and here the poet and Dorothy stayed in November 1805, a visit Dorothy recorded in her *Journal of a Mountain Ramble*. The way we go updale she referred to as "the path which goes from house to house", and described the charming fellside scenery through which it ran—"two or three times it took us through some of those copses or groves that cover every little hillock". She saw it most gloriously garbed in autumn. The colours of November flame upon the knoll across from the cottage, there is a golden splendour on fell slope and the most brilliant colours of autumn's palette are upon the rowans and birches in the gills which take numerous waterfalls and tumbling becks down to Goldrill Beck. The dale completely captured the Wordsworths with its beauty. Here the poet "pitched upon the spot where he should like to build a house better than in any other he had ever seen". In 1805 they had not settled finally in the Grasmere valley; they even went so far as to go from Patterdale to see Mr. Wilkinson of Yanwath about effecting the purchase of the chosen site for them. It was here during breakfast on November 10th that their host's maid burst in upon them with news of the death of Nelson and the victory of Trafalgar, but when they went to the inn to verify the news and heard there "were great rejoicings in Penrith and all the bells were ringing", said Dorothy, "Then Nelson can't be dead!"

The houses by the track; lovely names they bear, Rooking, Crook-a-beck, Beckstones. They all take shelter against the fell, they all face west to the dale; from their side windows they can watch the grey coiling snake of Kirkstone Pass and the tiny moving cars and coaches upon it—just as the first owners kept an eye on the coming of strangers. Once they watched for raiders; in the time of Jacobite rebellion they saw flocks and herds being driven along this dale to be hidden in lonely and secret hollows away from danger. Crook-a-beck is a typical lakeland farm, very old, with thick walls, heavy roof, and inside with its crooked doors and tilted floors and queer little staircases, so many steps up and steps down, it might almost be the crooked house of the rhyme. Once it had its old court cupboard built into the wall, but previous owners removed it. It is sad when this happens. The partition wall cupboards, the kists and spice cupboards, the inside walls of plank and muntin, the floors of smooth slates, the grey roofs and cylindrical chimneys—some with their "witch seats" above them, are among the most attractive features of lakeland rural architecture. At Crook-a-beck from the south window in the kitchen you can see the deep V of the pass and the cloud-play across the surrounding mountains. From the door, above the farmyard noises you can hear the mewing of hawks and watch birds hovering above the crags.

A walker along this way to Kirkstone Pass goes by Beckstones Farm and the track, now a green turf-floored " lonning ", continues most delightfully by becks, and over becks. In white spray of falls the water ousel—Beck Bibby or Jenny Dooker, to give her Cumbrian names—bobs and curtsies; she is seen here when the " green spray springs ", and in autumn when the Midas touch is on the gill-side trees, and there is a blaze on the fells from stream to sky-line. Later the lonning narrows between ancient boulder-built walls dappled with moss and lichens. Its course is still direct, southwards. Low Hartsop is its goal, a

OLD GALLERY—HARTSOP

hamlet which is so near the highway yet has preserved so much of its ancient peace. Here by Hayes Water Beck is a succession of old houses and farms, some with perfect wooden galleries projecting from the upper floors, some with vestiges of them. The spinning gallery in my sketch is an antique addition of the most picturesque, and forms part of a dwelling as exciting inside as it is on the outside. At the upper end of the hamlet is the gate opening to the lovely dale which brings down Hayes Water Beck from the tarn of that name. Immediately the loiterer feels he is in another world; the breezes sing through the rowans by a one-arched bridge, the beck chatters between its rocky walls, and birds call out of the clouds chasing over the purple screes at the gill head. Silent and deserted now, this dale was once a place of lead mining; the miners lived in cottages which are such charming homes. "It is lovely always—all the year round," said a woman I met at the lane end waiting for the arrival of the butcher's van. Low Hartsop is not so isolated now. Tradesmen's vans "deliver"; buses have their terminus at the road-end near Brothers Water so that even Penrith, which at one time must have seemed so far away, is now brought nearer.

And now back to the track at Crook-a-beck near which a path starts to climb the fells behind the farm. Looking up it disappears on the sky-line. Climbing, we come to the top of Stonebarrow Gill and on the heights, a place of reeds and rushes, boggy pools and turf-clad hillocks, is the Chapel in the Hause.

What a spot to linger in. Only the thought of the long journey to Penrith acts as a spur. With so little expense of energy we

BOARDALE HAUSE

have won the tops and have the world outstretched below us—so many delicious dales, so many head-in-cloud mountains. When there was a chapel here at the head of many mountain passes the fell folk must have been served by some itinerant priest. Nothing is left of the chapel now. It was no more than a fragmentary ruin in 1805 when Dorothy Wordsworth heard of the experiences of an old man who found shelter among its stones when caught here in a storm when gathering peats, lying here all night.

A guide post, a drunken post supported by a pile of stones, shows the meeting of the several routes from different dales. Each one is a lure. Boardale is the first, a green groove cradling utter peace. Bannerdale, the second, seems to wrap an even deeper solitude in its arms, and both open out to frame the blue middle reaches of Ullswater and a vista of distant blue mountains between their ridges. Both carry paths, then little lanes, down to the lake at Howtown, but once up we are not so eager to drop to valley level, attractive though the patchwork of fields undoubtedly is. We wander over the reedy rushy heights, our path little clearer than a sheep trod—hearing only the tinkle of waterdrops and rills, the plashy sounds of tiny streams taking movement from their springs, the breeze in the brackens, the thin bleat from a sheep, a hoarse croak from a raven, a hawk mewing on the wing, and we strike the green path over the turf of Beda Fell. Now we stride along between the two deep dales, seeing very little sign of man's handiwork. Bannerdale might be a valley in a lost land. Then the first straggling walls appear, the first intaken land; we see green paths threading the dale floor below us, and in one is a man; we hear his sweet, clear, piercing whistle as he calls his dog, and in a trice Bannerdale becomes part of this world. The glacial ice was the graving tool which smoothed and shaped the dale head slopes; the Romans knew the scene much as we see it, as they marched along their ridge road on the far side of this valley, along Ystryd, High Street, making north for the fort at Brougham, or south for Ambleside or Kendal. In mediæval times this spacious region was a great hunting forest where the red deer were the privileged denizens of the wild. They still roam here.

When we finally descend to valley level, a track gradually losing height on the rock-strewn fellside, the first building is Dale Head, an unusual-looking farm which was once a hunting lodge for the Hazells of Dalemain; it has a frontage supported on huge stone pillars, and a projecting roof. From the wide windows the ladies watched their menfolk going out to the Hunt, deer-stalking in the Forest of Martindale. The sound of a horn must sound very well indeed among these echoing mountains. "It is still heard once a year," wrote Dorothy Wordsworth, commenting that the day of festivity was hardly one for the poor deer, the most ancient and original inhabitants of Martindale.

It was a farmer of Martindale, Jack Wilson by name, who was positively the last to see fairies in Westmorland. This is such a vale of enchantment his story does not seem entirely incredible. He had been to the inn and had fallen sound asleep by the lane side; suddenly out of the silence of the dale came sweet music and a chorus of tiny voices and, waking, what did Jack see but a band of little men, not knee high, climbing a ladder into the sky, disappearing from sight, where he could not say, but he would tell his cronies in later years, "Men will never see their like again."

ST. MARTIN'S CHURCH

Dalehead, Thranghow, Henhow—pretty names, though the last has sinister memories and a ghost of a poor girl who once lived here, was seduced by a clergyman and given by him a draught of physic which proved so potent it did more than he intended, killing both the girl and her unborn child.

Henhow, along the lane by Howe Grain, over Christy Bridge, and we come to the old church of St. Martin, patron of the forest folk of Martin's dale, with its " base ring of mossy wall and its single yew tree "—a simple house of God built to endure and impressive as a greater edifice, borrowing dignity from age and sublimity from the mountains about it. A newer church stands not far away, but it is the old one we remember when the name of Martindale is spoken.

A mile of lane and the lakeside is reached, and three miles of lake-edge road, as attractive as any in the Lakeland region, go to Pooley Bridge. From it I have seen many memorable sights—once a spiralling waterspout racing across the lake from Oldchurch to Sandwick during a raging storm, once a cormorant fishing, and, once only, the antlers of a stag moving steadily across the lake, this in autumn when Martindale stags are known to swim over to Gowbarrow during rutting season. A century ago travellers used to watch the fishermen of Sandwick netting shoals of fish called skellies, which were a sort of freshwater herring. Wordsworth once saw fishermen drawing their nets ashore " and hundreds of fish were leaping in their prison ".

Ullswater has one scrap of mythology, the tale of a bridge-building giant who had big ideas for erecting a noble bridge of a single span from shore to shore. He built his piers and waited for his wife who acted as builder's mate to bring stones for the arch. But alas, the plans of giants as well as men gang aft agley. As she jumped across the lake the weight of stones broke her brat-string and all the stones fell into deep water. In disgust the giant gave up his attempt. And which rocky promontories were the piers he built? They are anybody's guess.

Following the lake shore there is nothing to hint at the prehistory and the relics of the distant past lingering in the fells above us. Nearing Pooley Bridge, a narrow lane joins the road from

Howtown; it comes from a farm, Roe Head, where begin tracks into the great silences of Moor Divock. Stone Circles, Tumuli, Standing Stones—all marks of prehistory—are thick upon the moor, not so clear perhaps as in the eighteenth century when West wrote of a "large karn of stones and near it the remains of a small circus; ten stones of which are still erect. A little farther on are the vestiges of a larger one of 22 paces by 25. All the stones except the pillar are removed." One called The Cockpit stands where High Street, coming arrow-straight out of the mountains, is crossed by the Askham-Pooley Bridge track. Where the Heltondale track crosses the Askham track is White Raise—"rais" or "hrais" is a name signifying an ancient mound—and a regular cemetery of prehistoric Cumbrians lies at the cross-roads and along the tracks. There is atmosphere up on these wild open heights. I felt it deeply on an autumn evening when I crossed Moor Divock on a walk from the Shap road, from Lowther and Askham to Pooley Bridge. I shall not easily forget it.

Many of the eighteenth-century tourists knew Lowther, for its park and castle were among the show places of Westmorland in Georgian times—and earlier, for, as we saw, Celia Fiennes paid the Lowthers an early morning visit in 1698. Those bound for Pooley Bridge, possibly through the advice of local countryfolk, discovered the old tracks over the fells, a very short cut from Askham to Ullswater foot. Walkers nowadays, leaving the long distance buses at Lowther road end, make this most dramatic approach to Lakeland—as I did one glorious November day. From the word "Go" I was dazzled with glories—the trees were aflame, the fells glowed with orange-tawny splendour; the air was soft, the light golden too. The day was so fair I would have declared with conviction to anyone who asked, that November was certainly the best of all months for walking through the Lake country.

Lowther village—the seventeenth-century Old Town—is a perfect picture, but part of a dream too good to be true. Its cottages surround grassy squares, flaming creepers cover the walls, flowers grow about the doors and rooks call above its background of tall trees. A few minutes from A6, but it might well be miles away. Linking it with Lowther New Town (which is not at all new but early Victorian and a most dignified, restrained and select sort of place, at the edge of the castle gardens and home of Lowther estate employees) is a tree tunnel, the sun like fire licking the foliage of the splendid beeches, elms and oaks which enclose it.

The castle is empty, a gaunt ruin standing in its vast park—a silent witness to past greatness. These green acres interspersed with noble trees now form a tourist attraction, the Lowther Wild Life Park. Part of the Deer Park, where large herds once roamed, is under cultivation, large tracks of woodland and copses are gone, so that the landscape has changed character. A golden glory was in the park, on the wooded limestone scars by the banks of the Lowther river—how glorious it was to see the dale from the quiet graveyard which overlooks the country—and down by Askham Bridge were the most brilliant colours of all.

Askham has a fine old church at the Lowther edge. When I rested within and faced the east windows I looked twice at the rich hues within the stone tracery. Was it stained glass? No. Askham did well to put clear glass in its windows. No artist could use a more brilliant palette than nature's! The most rich colours at autumn's disposal had been squandered on the wooded Lowther banks and the east window framed them. Hall windows and vicarage windows look on this beauty, too. As for Askham village, it climbs half a mile from riverside to fell edge and has beauty every yard at its command. I place Askham among the fairest of English villages. I was loath to leave it but the fells called—a green fell track invited me upwards to Moor Divock, and a vague path thrown across wild acres of rust-red, tawny, crimson, pulled me away. On Moor Divock the winds speak of strange things. Here one walks with prehistory. I was alone with the past. With every step it came nearer until at the highest point I could imagine in the wind the cries of men who long ago inhabited the heights, who worshipped their gods in sacred plots defined by stone circles, who buried their dead where the wind could rage and the rains beat upon their mounds. Some places hold longer than others the atmosphere of primeval times. Moor Divock is one.

Striding down to meet the direct path from Askham comes the Roman High Street, a wide green ribbon against the browns of the fell. A lonely guide post shows the meeting of the moorland ways. Here I turned northwards. I could see one stretch of the lake below. Pooley Bridge was hidden from sight. My track descended quickly, turf-clad at first then rutted deep by tractors, going down to the farms at Roe Head to meet the lane to the lake head. How quiet it was and still! The only movement was the hovering of a hawk's wings high above the fell, dangling as if held by an invisible string. No cattle grazed the in-pastures, no flocks were to be seen on the open heafs as in other months. And in the dale—" the sedge is withered by the lake—and no birds sing ".

I think the old gods of our remote ancestors stride over these empurpled heights on quiet evenings, and when storms rage across the mountains they drape themselves in cloud-wrack or hurl thunderbolts as did the Nordic deities worshipped by our Norse forbears. Here we feel very near the heart of old Cumbria.

Not far away, as the crow flies, low by the River Eamont, was

DACRE CASTLE

enacted long ago one of the first pages of the recorded history of Cumbria. Dacre is the place to track it down, a village two miles from the lake foot, written Dacore in the chronicles of the Venerable Bede, who set down that there by the " trickling stream " was a monastic house. Nothing remains of this, but there is in the church a carved stone to keep in memory the historic meeting here of three kings—Athelstan the Great, victor of Brunanburgh, conqueror of the Northumbrians, the Welsh, the Scots of Strathclyde and the Cumbrians therein, and the invading armies of Ireland and Scandinavia—Constantine, King of Scotland, and Owain Gwynedd of North Wales. Here in A.D. 926, soon after their defeat, they signed a treaty with the King of Wessex and some stone carver of the time recorded—as my sketch shows—an incident which followed. The Fall of Man was a most popular subject with early Christians so he gave us a picture of Adam and Eve beneath the Tree of Knowledge in Eden, and the Serpent coiled round its trunk. He carved an animal which was probably intended for a stag and another lively beast above—but the main object of his handiwork was the coming together of Constantine and Athelstan—they are shown shaking hands. Soon afterwards Constantine's son was baptized a Christian.

In the village they tell you that Dacre Castle has The Room of the Three Kings. Maybe the traditional site of the meeting was here, but the castle was not built till four centuries and more later. And a splendid hall it is, a massive, single, upstanding keep with corner turrets, rather like Castle Bolton in Wensleydale, without any outer walls or defences. Now it is a dwelling with green fields about it, a place of settled calm, with wagtails sporting in the stream near by and ducks paddling through the tanglement of meadow-sweet and crane's-bill on summer days. It was not always so peaceful. The Dacres were among the belligerent gentry of the border stories, so were the Musgraves and other families connected with the place. The adjoining village church has relics of the lords of the castle. There are the curious stone bears hugging posts—rather like the bear and billet—possibly a badge of the Musgraves; there is a recumbent effigy of Ranulph de Musgrave, cross-legged, in red sandstone; there are memorials to local families of later days—to the Hazells long resident at Dalemain down the valley, to the Salmonds of the mansion called Waterfoot, and in the churchyard fine calligraphy on metal plates inset upon soft red sandstone gravestones. And, of course, there are the scraps and fragments of pre-Norman carvings.

THE DACRE STONE

The village itself is charming, out of sight of the lake, within the arms of the hills, its homely hostelry, the Horse and Farrier, as pleasant a place of call to-day as it was in the eighteenth century. The Wordsworths knew it well, and "the very pleasant walk over Dacre Beck, over miserable stepping stones" to Park House where their in-laws the Hutchinsons moved in 1805. The poet and his wife and sister often came here, and the little Wordsworths too when whooping cough was rife at Grasmere. They knew the delightful by-ways to Hutton John, the paths to Dalemain and Barton and to Yanwath—off the beaten track to twentieth-century travellers, but much used a century and more ago.

BETWEEN POOLEY BRIDGE AND EAMONT BRIDGE

At Pooley Bridge, with the mountains and the lake behind us, we might well think we have said good-bye to all that is most grand and beautiful in the tour of Lakeland. Perhaps so, but when we are no longer concerned with beauty spots we have time to take in other features of the landscape. Behind us lies Ullswater and Beauty; ahead is the Eamont valley—and History and Romance. The road passing through Barton, Tirril and Yanwath is in itself pleasant, through farmlands which increase in richness the nearer we draw to Penrith, but the hamlets and villages, the wayside farms and gracious old houses are the main features, not one being without its own treasures of architecture. Exteriors give little indication of the fine heritage of old craftsmanship they have within them.

Curious travellers of the past commented on little by this roadside apart from the conical hill, Dunmallet, which overlooks Pooley Bridge so dramatically—"a fine pointed hill covered with wood", wrote Thomas Gray, which had been planted by old Mr. Hazell of Dalemain "who always lived at home and delighted in planting". He climbed it by a broad avenue—as later tourists were advised to do, by West and others, to see the fine views of the lake, and descended by a path—"that was only not perpendicular"—to Barton Bridge. West called Dunmallet "the greatest ornament of the lake" and described the remains of a Roman fort atop—110 paces by 37 surrounded by a foss, which obviously guarded the lake and the pass of the Eamont. When the Wordsworths stayed with friends, the Clarksons, at Eusemere—just beyond the lake foot—Dorothy climbed Dunmallet in light

KIRKBARROW

snow for the sake of the view. It is still as interesting a shape and still well clad in trees, loveliest to see before November gales strip them of their multi-coloured foliage.

Roughly two miles from Pooley Bridge is Barton with its scattered farms and its fine old church. One farm is at the wayside, Kirkbarrow, the subject of my sketch, with a most unusual porch. I can well believe the house was there in mediæval times though only the sixteenth- and seventeenth-century architectural styles show to the passer-by. Two equally interesting farms are hidden from the road, behind the church, Church Farm and Glebe Farm.

Barton is such a very English name; scores of them are scattered through the land, their meaning usually " corn farm " and outlying grange. I found this Barton but a step from the highroad, " the Tirril turnpike ", one summer afternoon. In a moment I was carried back down the centuries. A step from the highway—peace and quiet; through the sunny graveyard and into the cool, shadowed church—and six hundred years had rolled back. This is among the finest village churches on the fringe of Lakeland; it has a twelfth-century tower, square and strong, a structure on double arches spanning the nave and forming a dark tunnel-like passage beneath—a most unusual feature, an architectural puzzle now and doubtless an architectural problem to the late Norman builders who erected it, and the fourteenth-century masons who strengthened it. All who worked upon the fabric wrought with an eye for permanence—and incidentally for beauty too. In the south chapel with its lovely stone carving I noticed memorials to Wordsworths recalling that they were a local family —a John Wordsworth of Penrith died 1819 and Anne in 1815.

The most touching epitaph in the church, couched in typical seventeenth-century style, was that of Francisca Dawes of Barton Kirk, who died in 1673 aged 23; it is on a brass plate near the east window.

> "At her appearance the noone sun
> Blush'd and shrunke because was quite undone.
> In her concentr'd did all graces dwell.
> God pluckt my rose yt He might take a smell."

BARTON CHURCH

A passing farmer directed my attention in the churchyard to a most fascinating bygone—the Coach House and stables built against the north aisle wall. Long ago when parishioners rode to church, the men with their womenfolk pillion behind them, it was necessary to find stabling for their mounts whilst they were at service. Here are stalls for six horses and doubtless late-comers would tie up at the church gate. There is a small midden by the stable, and mounting steps for the less agile. None is used now—for none comes to Barton Kirk on horseback and the sexton keeps all his digging tools in the old building. The farmer made sure I did not overlook the method by which the slates were held in place under the roofing. Bones, not nails, were used by Barton builders long ago and the sheep shanks, with which the roof bristles, seem to last for ever.

North of the church a lane passes to the farms beyond and ends there. Both farms are of great age, and linked by huge barns and byres. From the first—with dressed stones by doors and windows painted black and white, and a number of dated stones over house door and on barn walls all telling of building done by seventeenth- and eighteenth-century Dawes, an archway leads into the yard of the second farm, which appears to be even more venerable. Down how many centuries have men cultivated these rich acres which slope to the Eamont? There is an air of settled age round us. Passing through cornfields where the air throbs with the sound of reaper and binder on August days, paths make for the river and a footbridge into the Park of the Hazells of Dalemain, again land cultivated and cared for down the centuries. Dalemain in turn joins on to land belonging to the owners of Dacre Castle, another historic site and building by a beck which is a tributary of the Eamont. I often walk from Dacre Castle by Dalemain to Barton, Sockbridge and Penrith when I wish to avoid roads.

A mile north of Barton the highroad comes to Tirril, with inn and pretty cottages round a triangular green, and a little church—a clustered village where the Roman High Street after descending straight from fell and mountain strikes across the fields to ford the Eamont at the fort of Brougham. Tirril must have seen a great deal of traffic in its time—for nearly nineteen centuries. The "lost" road was once kept trodden enough, and that long after Roman recall in the fifth century. It was "Y Strata"—a metalled "street" as opposed to a soft, peaty track, with careful construction comprising four layers of material. Sections excavated on Loadpot Hill, over a mountain ridge, show a foundation of large quarried stones two feet thick, with a layer of peats eight inches thick above, then nine inches of gravel and a final surfacing of sods or turf. In mediæval times the road was attributed to the Britons and known as Brettes Streete. Maybe the Scots used it and sections were dubbed Scots Rake. It was a land boundary and recorded in documents and disputes. Drovers herded their cattle along the route between Penrith and Ambleside, farmers dragged their loaded peat sleds along it, wearing down the road in softer sections into a deep, rutty groove. Because shepherds from many valleys could climb up to the mountain meeting-place—above Swindale, Mardale, Kentmere, Martindale and Troutbeck valley—the Roman Road became a recognized "Meet" for exchange of strayed sheep, for games and wrestling matches, and Race Course Hill—Loadpot Hill—was known throughout Cumberland and Westmorland for its fell-top races. Tirril, the only community between Troutbeck and Brougham, shared in the life of the road.

Before the Tirril turnpike was made, travellers wandered by a narrow lane from Barton into the hamlet of Sockbridge. The lane is still there, but so little used it is almost choked in summer with high grasses, nettles, Canterbury bells, purple crane's-bill and trailing wild roses which, with the brambles, try to hold you back. The old way first enters Thorpe, Sockbridge's smaller neighbour, a place of sweet seclusion, standing high to look over the tree-tops to the long, blue Pennine fells. The lane pushes through the flowers and trees to a green tunnel, at the end of which is Sockbridge—a half-forgotten place, with charming houses; one dated 1699 has clipped yews, others have white walls and gay touches of colour at door and window—a feature which becomes obvious once we leave the heart of Lakeland. Like so many villages here is one which does not care if traffic has by-passed it for nearly two hundred years. The inhabitants need not touch the highroad when they go to Penrith, but I think most prefer to take the bus from Tirril rather than follow Eamont-side field paths—such a short cut to Red Hills and Penrith Castle.

Less than a mile from Tirril the road passes under the main-line railway to Scotland—a stirring sight to see the Royal Scot speed by—then for contrast to turn left to the place where a house of great antiquity keeps watch over the Eamont ford, though it has known for centuries that no one will cross, neither friend, nor the foe against which its defences were designed. Any place-name ending in "wath" tells that it stands by a ford—we have Wath, Aldwath, Slape Wath, Langwathby—and here Yanwath. In 1323, at a time of fiercest border warfare and conflict with the Scots, John de Sutton erected his fortified tower for watch and ward, shelter and refuge, as north-country land-owners had erected others at points along the same invasion route. We have seen those at Levens, Sizergh, Burneside and Cunswick, at Wraysholm, Cowmire Hall and Kentmere. In each case the first stone pele—offering but cramped quarters—was added to later, a commodious hall being built alongside, a strong wall raised to enclose the courtyard and an entrance gate and archway to admit friends and keep out foes. The foes were the Scots—and too often they came uncomfortably near the Eamont ford at Yanwath.

After the Suttons the powerful Threlkelds gained possession of the hall and lands. An heiress married Thomas, Lord Dudley, one of the family of Northumberlands who in championing the cause of Lady Jane Grey lost so much. One day when I came along from the main road to wander round the gardens and courtyard, to make my drawing of the Hall, I busied my thoughts with a great deal more besides. It is a most exciting house, with lovely peeps through old archways, uneven light upon cobbled yards and red sandstone pavements, signs of great strength in walls and heavy buttresses, lighter touches of grace and elegance in turrets

YANWATH HALL

and trefoil-headed windows. The sun rests softly on the tower, the stonework of delicate pink-tinged sandstone.

"Mary Queen of Scots slept here when she fled from the Scots," a man digging in a potato patch informed me. He broke into my thoughts, concerned at the moment with Dorothy Wordsworth. I wonder why she did not write more fully of the Hall when she called here in 1805.

She and William, eager to buy the site for the house in Patterdale, came to Park House—where relations of Mrs. Wordsworth lived—a farm between Dacre Castle and Dalemain, and the next morning they went down the valley to cross the Eamont at the ford of Yanwath. There they found Thomas Wilkinson at work in one of his fields—but of the Hall, and the superb views of the mountains seen from its windows, and of the dramatic sight the battlemented tower makes on approaching Yanwath, she makes no mention. Neither does she write of Dacre Castle, equally impressive in the Eamont landscape.

Three years later Thomas Wilkinson, a Quaker, was host to Coleridge for some months. The poet had been cutting down his intake of opium and his health and mind were so improved that he was ready to exert himself in the publication of a new magazine, *The Friend.* For six months it prospered—then Coleridge gave up the work, left Yanwath, and his Grasmere friends, and his family with Southey at Keswick, making a break with all his Lakeland connections. Yanwath saw him in one of his most cheerful periods; they were very rare.

A wayside inn near the Hall allows no one to pass by without giving it due notice; the Old Yanwath Gate Inn—with its sign a hanging gate and these lines on a wall:

> "This gate hangs well and hinders none.
> Refresh and Pay and Travel on."

Short, sweet and to the point.

Across the way a hole i' th' wall arch shows a path going off across the pastures to Eamont Bridge, the route for all who go to Penrith on foot, and only half a mile to Mayburgh, that great prehistoric enclosure about which writers have been puzzling for many a year. It is on the right of the path, the river on the left. Climb the green encircling bank and you look into the arena with a single standing stone in the centre—a place of "remote antiquity and doubtful use", says West, who adds that Mr. Brougham of Brougham Hall saw that the monolith, which was visible from his house, was kept whitewashed. West was inclined to think with Pennant that Mayburgh had been "a supreme consistory of druidical administration", and "a place of study and contemplation for the instruction of pupils in the mysteries of the druidical religion". A centre of early religion or a place for law-giving, Mayburgh is still a site where anyone looking inwards upon it must ponder. So is King Arthur's Round Table which is at the road end, a mile beyond Yanwath inn, where our road from Ullswater meets A6.

King Arthur's Table is not what it used to be, we are told. Road-making has cut into and mangled its original shape. Enough remains to show that it was indeed round with a central platform surrounded by a trench and the whole enclosed by high banks. "A place of public exhibition for martial exercises"—a likely use for the enclosure, but whether or no Arthur and his knights ever assembled there to watch or partake in deeds of prowess we do not know. What a place for wrestling matches—or village sports—or country dancing—or open air theatre performances! I could think of many uses to which the old site could be put to-day. As I made my drawing children and dogs were racing around and rolling on the grass.

Here at Eamont village and Eamont Bridge the tour of the Lakes is over. We are back on the eastern edge of the Lakeland area on the same road from which we started out. Penrith is a mile away over the river in Cumberland. Kendal is 27 miles south along the highroad, a road I travelled and explored in *Lancashire-Westmorland Highway*.

KING ARTHUR'S ROUND TABLE—EAMONT

If we count this journey's end we are only following the rule of the centuries. To the ancient people of Cumbria it was a desired end to which they had come from the mountain country, through morass and wild wasteland, fording many rivers, fighting against many difficulties; we do not know if they saw great beauty in their surroundings as we do, but they certainly had a feeling for dramatic effect. None of their tribal meeting-places but have impressive sites and settings. Where they forgathered we stand and we must feel something of the spirit and awe and reverence with which they endowed them.

Here at the fords of Lowther and Eamont Roman legionaries, weary from their mountain route march, halted and, looking back at the horrid heights, sighed with relief. High Street, mists, blizzards, gales—and local guerillas—good-bye to them for a while. A mile away was the fort of Brocavum, and the security of their fort's defences. They saw no beauty in the journey behind them.

What of the Angles who settled in waves during the seventh century? Most of them chose to live on the outer fringe of the land of lakes. They left it to the invaders of a later period, the Norsemen, to probe deep into the hills; they saw in high mountains overhanging long lakes something akin to the fjords of their homeland and turning towards the dale heads felt that here they could live content—fishing, herding their flocks and cattle, farming in their own way. They must have seen beauty here which found an answer in their hearts; they stayed and their descendants, and those of the native Celts, dwell in Lakeland to-day.

The Normans thought little of the Lakes; some received lands therein, but many passed them to monastic establishments of their foundation, leaving it to abbot and brethren to civilize the boorish and uncivilized folk. The mark of the Norman is most evident in the fat lands of the Lakeland margin. They came with their servants along the roads we have travelled; at Eamont they thought appreciatively of the towns on the roads north to Scotland, of the great castles and fine estates in the wide plains beyond Penrith.

We might trace from early times the history of travel on the roads through the Lakes, but we should be required to read on many centuries before we came to Lakeland travel considered as an end in itself—for pure pleasure and joy in recollection. I have in this book quoted from the writing of many who did count the lovely moments in every mile—as we do. The eighteenth century was the turning point. Even the writers of a prosaic book on the agriculture of Cumberland felt impelled in 1797 to extol the "height, ruggedness, the sublime assemblage of mountains", and the scenes of lake and mountain they declared "few other places, if any, in the world can equal". This was a long cry from the "horrid mountains" which repelled writers like Defoe and gave the jitters to travellers earlier in the same century.

Curious travellers come from all classes nowadays. Among the "Seven Lakes" tourists in their *de luxe* coaches are many as curious as the motorists boxed in their cars. I think the remark of a hard-working weaver from one of the darker industrial towns sums up the general feeling of to-day. She was commenting on the houses and people dwelling alongside the Ambleside-Rydal-Grasmere road. "There's some folks," she said with envy in her voice, "as has their 'eaven on earth."

Oh, those thrice fortunate people who have their lovely houses under Loughrigg, along Grasmere vale, their lawns laved by lake water, their rock gardens climbing to the coppice fringe of the fells; wno gaze from their own empyrean heights over the vale of Keswick and Borrowdale!. Let us hope they get their heaven in after-life too.

How well writers who are not English—or even British—have got under the skin of Lakeland. A friend of mine, a Lancastrian, holidaying in Switzerland, stood by Lake Geneva one evening admiring the scene in company with two Americans. They talked and when they discovered from whence he came they were astounded that one living so near the English lakes should wish to go in search of others. In their tour they had visited Lakeland, had passed through Europe and with a month still to spend were returning to England—"because we have seen nothing to equal your lakes, nothing so exquisitely beautiful". It is very heart-warming to find such admiration and appreciation.

Once I met an Indian student in Borrowdale. He had been spending his long vacation from college walking through the Lakes and when I talked with him his delight in the scene around us was evident.

"Judged by our mountains of India yours are very small," he said, "like our Ghats, but how different—how green, how very green! I have walked across them and I have been constantly refreshed and inspired. Sometimes I have found myself singing —no words, no music, but just an upwelling of my inner happiness."

With Chiang Yee, the Silent Traveller, who walked almost without speaking through Lakeland, "joy born out of that tranquillity in my mind will render unforgettable my years in England". Karel Capek, the Czech writer, in his *Letters from England,* at times experienced what we all feel—such sweetness and peace that we are "uneasy with happiness". Even the Cumbrian flocks are to him like "the souls of the blessed in heaven" for they graze heavenly pastures, and as for the cows—"to be a cow in the Lake District is a great favour which falls only to the lot of the most sacred and worthy among all creatures".

For nearly five centuries this corner of England had its meed of praise. What Michael Drayton wrote is still true enough—

> "The lofty hills though rough yet smile upon their beholders, spread with sheep and cattle, the valleys stored with corn and grass sufficient, the sea affordeth great store of fish, and the land is overspread with a great variety of fowles."

The lofty hills smile on their beholders. The shining lakes mirror peace. The tourist comes and goes—and each one is better for having travelled through this region of such diverse loveliness. Such beauty, as Wordsworth said with truth:

> "——cannot be portrayed
> By words, nor by the pencil's silent skill,
> But is the property of him alone
> Who hath beheld it, noted it with care
> And in his mind recorded it with love."

To sum up in 1972 after nearly twenty years. Possession is a state of mind; thousands of outsiders feel they have a stake in Lakeland. Yet those who live within, and those who love it from without, do not always see eye to eye.

Neither do the three counties of the Lakeland Planning Board, the largest single landowners the National Trust, Friends of the Lakes, Council for the Protection of Rural England and the countless protectionists and preservationists always agree with the local councils, the residents, road planners and water authorities.

Any plan which constitutes a threat to its beauty rouses defenders everywhere; I was asked to sign "Hands off Ullswater" in Grantchester, Cambridge! I had already offered the "defence committee" use of what I had written of the lake. My books were quoted by Philip Barnes of C.P.R.E. when Longsleddale was in danger. At such times all are eager to help.

The greatest threats are from road transport, by "Murder by fast and heavy traffic" in Lord Chorley's words; and from thirsty cities with a too wasteful use of tapwater. Selling gallons of water by the meter, more de-salination, and Lakeland would be saved. Smaller threats: outboard motors in quiet waters, too many water skiers—both interfering with the pleasure of rowing and sailing; over-use of pedestrian tracks by horse riders and pony trekkers, churning them to mud and destroying fords over becks.

Tree planting and felling is now being done with care and consideration of hill contours. Camps and caravan sites have been "contained". Nowhere in England is beauty so well guarded. As a precious heritage it must be.

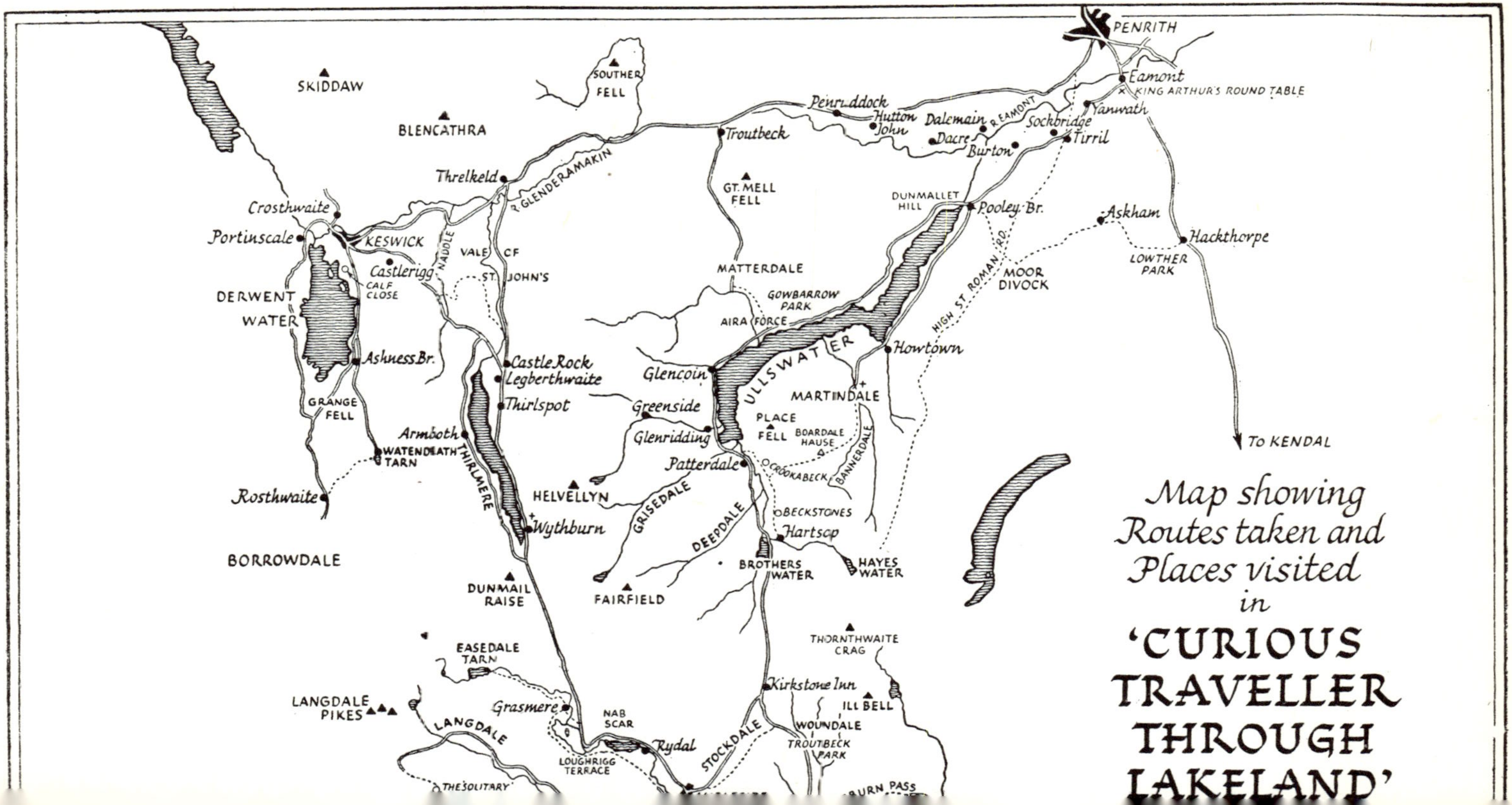

Map showing Routes taken and Places visited in
'CURIOUS TRAVELLER THROUGH LAKELAND'
PENRITH
Eamont
KING ARTHUR'S ROUND TABLE
Yanwath
Tirril
Sockbridge
R. EAMONT
Dalemain
Dacre
Burton
Hutton John
Penruddock
Troutbeck
SKIDDAW
SOUTHER FELL
BLENCATHRA
Threlkeld
R. GLENDERAMAKIN
GT. MELL FELL
Crosthwaite
Portinscale
KESWICK
Castlerigg
CALF CLOSE
NADDLE
VALE OF ST. JOHN'S
DERWENT WATER
Ashness Br.
GRANGE FELL
Castle Rock
Legberthwaite
Thirlspot
Armboth
WATENDLATH TARN
THIRLMERE
Rosthwaite
BORROWDALE
Wythburn
HELVELLYN
DUNMAIL RAISE
MATTERDALE
GOWBARROW PARK
AIRA FORCE
Glencoin
Greenside
Glenridding
Patterdale
GRISEDALE
DEEPDALE
FAIRFIELD
ULLSWATER
DUNMALLET HILL
Pooley Br.
Askham
Hackthorpe
LOWTHER PARK
MOOR DIVOCK
HIGH ST. ROMAN RD.
Howtown
MARTINDALE
PLACE FELL
BOARDALE HAUSE
CROOKABECK
BANNERDALE
BECKSTONES
Hartsop
BROTHERS WATER
HAYES WATER
TO KENDAL
THORNTHWAITE CRAG
Kirkstone Inn
ILL BELL
WOUNDALE
TROUTBECK PARK
STOCKDALE
EASEDALE TARN
Grasmere
NAB SCAR
Rydal
LOUGHRIGG TERRACE
LANGDALE PIKES
LANGDALE
THE SOLITARY

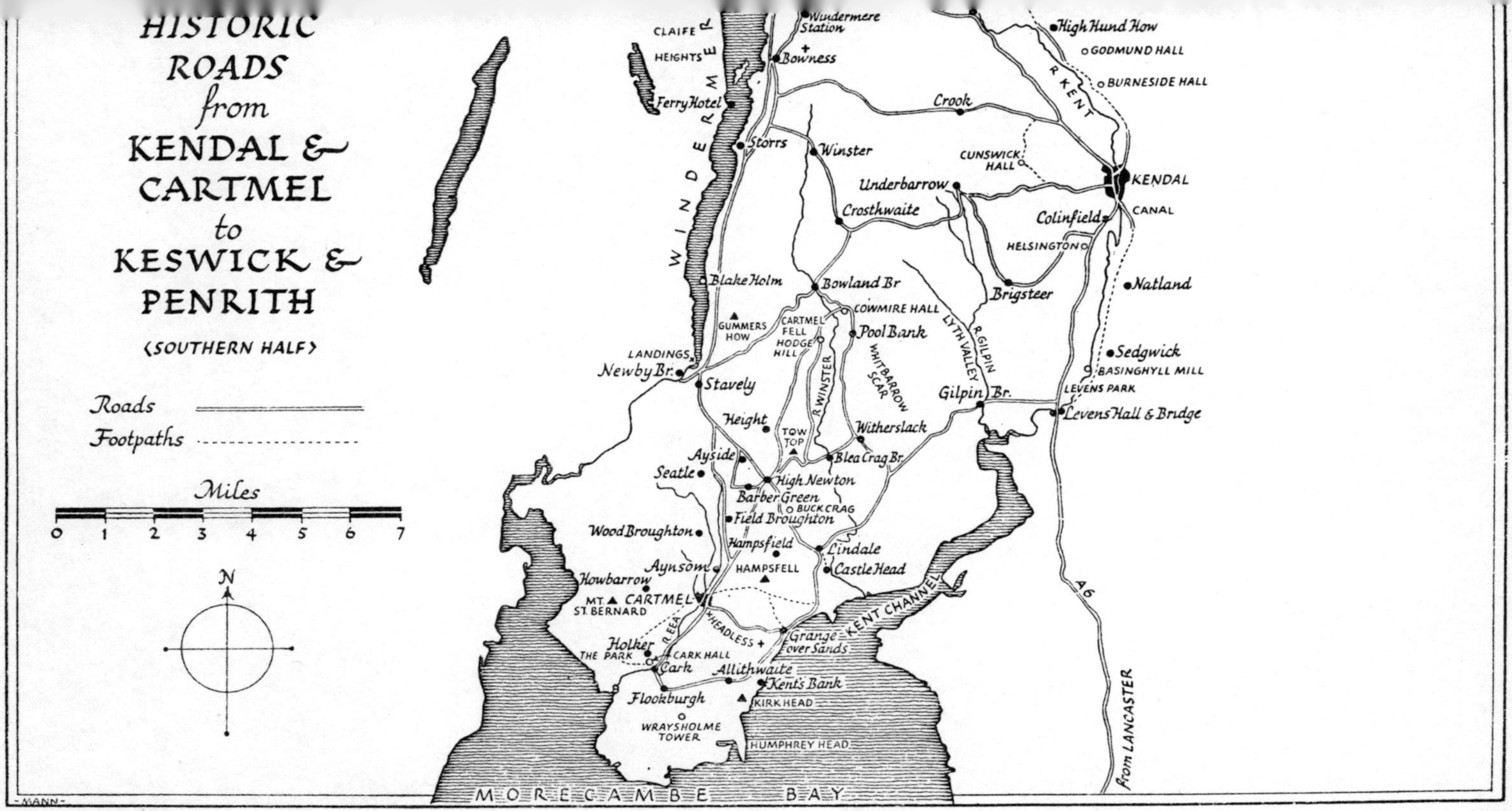

HISTORIC ROADS from KENDAL & CARTMEL to KESWICK & PENRITH
(SOUTHERN HALF)
Roads
Footpaths
Miles
0 1 2 3 4 5 6 7
N
CLAIFE HEIGHTS
Windermere Station
Bowness
Ferry Hotel
WINDERMERE
Storrs
Winster
Crook
High Hund How
GODMUND HALL
BURNESIDE HALL
R. KENT
CUNSWICK HALL
KENDAL
Underbarrow
CANAL
Crosthwaite
Colinfield
HELSINGTON
Blake Holm
Bowland Br
Natland
Brigsteer
COWMIRE HALL
GUMMERS HOW
CARTMEL FELL
Pool Bank
HODGE HILL
LYTH VALLEY
R. GILPIN
Sedgwick
BASINGHYLL MILL
LANDINGS
Newby Br.
Stavely
R. WINSTER
WHITBARROW SCAR
Gilpin Br.
LEVENS PARK
Levens Hall & Bridge
Height
TOW TOP
Witherslack
Ayside
Blea Crag Br.
Seatle
High Newton
Barber Green
BUCK CRAG
Field Broughton
Wood Broughton
Hampsfield
Lindale
Aynsom
HAMPSFELL
Castle Head
Howbarrow
A6
MT. ST. BERNARD
CARTMEL
R. EEA
HEADLESS +
Grange over Sands
KENT CHANNEL
Holker
THE PARK
CARK HALL
Cark
Allithwaite
Kent's Bank
Flookburgh
KIRK HEAD
WRAYSHOLME TOWER
HUMPHREY HEAD
from LANCASTER
MORECAMBE BAY
MANN

INDEX

Y